15 Compelling Reasons
to Choose Kamala Harris
Over Donald Trump

Copyright © 2024 by Janet Corder Heminger @ DL Corder Publishing

All rights reserved. No part of this publication may be reproduced in any form, or by any means, electronic or mechanical, including photocopying, recording, or any information browsing, storage, or retrieval system, without permission in writing from the author (jan@spokenwordengage.com).

First Printing
Cover Design: Janet Corder Heminger

Printed in the United States of America

Disclaimer:

This book is a work of political analysis and opinion. The author has made every effort to ensure the accuracy of the information contained herein at the time of writing. However, due to the rapidly changing nature of politics, some information may have become outdated by the time of publication.

The views and opinions expressed in this book are those of the author and do not necessarily reflect the official policy or position of any agency, organization, employer or company. The author is not affiliated with Kamala Harris, her campaign, or any political party.

This book is not authorized, endorsed, or sponsored by Kamala Harris, her campaign, or any political organization. It is an independent work of analysis and commentary.

The author and publisher are not responsible for any errors or omissions, or for the results obtained from the use of this information. All information in this book is provided "as is", with no guarantee of completeness, accuracy, timeliness or of the results obtained from the use of this information.

Readers are encouraged to verify any information contained herein and to seek professional advice where appropriate. The author and publisher disclaim any liability, loss, or risk incurred as a consequence, directly or indirectly, of the use and application of any of the contents of this book.

Table of Contents

Introduction

Chapter 1: Experience and Qualifications

Chapter 2: Leadership Style and Character

Chapter 3: Domestic Policy

Chapter 4: Economic Policy

Chapter 5: Social Issues

Chapter 6: Environmental Policy

Chapter 7: Foreign Policy

Chapter 8: Representation and Progress

Conclusion

Appendices

Senator Kamala Harris - Kavanaugh Confirmation Hearing Opening Statement - September 4, 2018

CNN September 6, 2018 - Kavanaugh Questioned On Capitol Hill - Kavanaugh Takes Pointed Questions - Sen. Harris Questions Kavanaugh

OPEN HEARING ON FOREIGN INFLUENCE OPERATIONS' USE OF SOCIAL MEDIA PLATFORMS - Kamala Harris

Introduction
America at a Crossroads

The United States finds itself at a pivotal moment in its history. The choice before the American people is not merely a selection between two individuals vying for the highest office in the land; it is a decision that will shape the trajectory of our nation for years, if not decades, to come. In this critical juncture, we are called upon to examine, with clear eyes and open minds, the candidates who seek to lead us through the challenges and opportunities that lie ahead.

On one side of the political arena stands Kamala Harris, a woman whose journey to this moment is as remarkable as it is inspiring. Born to immigrant parents - a Jamaican father and an Indian mother - Harris embodies the American dream in many ways. Her ascent from the daughter of civil rights activists to the first woman, first Black person, and first person of South Asian descent to hold the office of Vice President of the United States is a testament to both her own tenacity and the progress our nation has made. Yet, her story is far from complete, as she now seeks the presidency itself.

In the opposite corner, we find Donald Trump, a figure who needs little introduction to the American public. A businessman and reality television star turned politician, Trump's unconventional path to the presidency in 2016 and his subsequent term in office have left an indelible mark on American politics. His "America First" ideology and unorthodox approach to governance have energized his base while simultaneously polarizing the nation.

The contrast between these two candidates could not be more pronounced. Their backgrounds, experiences, policy positions, and visions for America's future diverge dramatically on almost every conceivable level. As voters, we are tasked with the weighty responsibility of looking beyond the surface-level narratives, digging deeper than sensationalized headlines, and truly understanding what each candidate represents and what their leadership would mean for our country.

This book aims to present a comprehensive and compelling case for why Kamala Harris deserves your vote. We will explore fifteen key reasons, examining her qualifications, policy proposals, leadership style, and vision for America. In doing so, we'll also contrast her positions with those of Donald Trump, providing a clear picture of the choice before us. However, it's crucial to note that this book is not intended to tell you how to vote. Rather, it's designed to provide you with well-researched, factual information to help inform your decision.

Before we delve into the specifics, it's important to understand the context in which this election is taking place. The United States, like much of the world, is grappling with a series of unprecedented challenges. The ongoing effects of the COVID-19 pandemic have exposed and exacerbated long-standing inequalities in our healthcare system, economy, and society at large. Climate change continues to pose an existential threat, with increasingly frequent and severe natural disasters serving as stark reminders of the urgency of this crisis. Racial tensions and calls for social justice have reached a boiling point, demanding meaningful action and reform. Meanwhile, on the global stage, America's role and influence are being questioned and challenged in ways not seen since the end of the Cold War.

It is against this backdrop that we must evaluate our potential leaders. We need to ask ourselves: Who is best equipped to navigate these turbulent waters? Who has the experience, the vision, and the character to not only address these immediate challenges but to chart a course towards a more prosperous, equitable, and sustainable future for all Americans?

As we examine the case for Kamala Harris, it's crucial to approach this evaluation with a critical and discerning eye. In today's age of information overload and "fake news," it's more important than ever to rely on credible sources, fact-check claims, and think critically about the information we consume. Throughout this book, we will strive to present accurate, verifiable information, and we encourage you to cross-reference and further investigate the points made.

Let's take a moment to consider the weight of the decision before us. The President of the United States is often referred to as the "leader of the free world," a title that speaks to the global influence and responsibility that comes with the office. The president's decisions impact not only the lives of over 330 million Americans but also have far-reaching consequences for people around the world. From economic policies that can trigger global market shifts to foreign policy decisions that can alter the balance of international relations, the ripple effects of presidential actions are immense.

Moreover, the president plays a crucial role in shaping the national narrative and setting the tone for public discourse. They have the power to unite or divide, to inspire or discourage, to promote understanding or fuel animosity. In an era of increasing polarization, the ability of a president to bridge divides and foster a sense of common purpose is more important than ever.

As we compare Kamala Harris and Donald Trump, it's essential to consider not just their stated policy positions, but also their leadership styles, their character, and their vision for America's role in the world. We must look at their track records, their ability to build and work with effective teams, their response to crises, and their capacity for growth and learning.

Kamala Harris brings to the table a wealth of experience in public service. Her career trajectory - from District Attorney of San Francisco to Attorney General of California, from U.S. Senator to Vice President - has given her a unique perspective on the challenges facing Americans at various levels of government. Her background in law enforcement and criminal justice reform positions her to address one of the most pressing issues of our time: the need for comprehensive police reform and the pursuit of racial justice.

Harris's time in the Senate, particularly her work on the Intelligence Committee, has provided her with valuable insights into national security matters and foreign policy challenges. As Vice President, she has been involved in high-level diplomatic engagements and policy discussions, further broadening her experience in international affairs.

On the domestic front, Harris has been a vocal advocate for healthcare reform, climate action, and economic policies aimed at supporting the middle class. Her proposed policies often focus on addressing systemic inequalities and promoting opportunity for all Americans, regardless of their background.

Donald Trump, on the other hand, came to the presidency with a very different set of experiences. His background in real estate and reality television informed a unique approach to governance, one that often prioritized showmanship and "deal-making" over traditional political processes. His presidency was marked by significant tax cuts, deregulation efforts, a hardline stance on immigration, and an "America First" foreign policy that often put him at odds with traditional U.S. allies.

Trump's supporters often point to his business acumen and outsider status as strengths, arguing that he brought a fresh perspective to Washington and wasn't beholden to established political interests. His critics, however, argue that his lack of political experience led to numerous missteps and a failure to fully grasp the complexities of governance.

As we compare these two candidates, it's crucial to look beyond personality and style to examine the substance of their proposals and the potential impacts of their policies. How would their approaches to healthcare affect access and affordability? What would their economic policies mean for job creation, income inequality, and the national debt? How would their stances on climate change and environmental regulation impact our planet and our economy? How would their foreign policy approaches affect America's standing in the world and our relationships with both allies and adversaries?

It's also important to consider the broader implications of their leadership. The president doesn't just implement policies; they also set priorities, shape the national conversation, and influence the direction of their political party. They nominate Supreme Court justices and other federal judges who can impact the interpretation of laws for generations. They have the power to issue executive orders, negotiate international agreements, and serve as commander-in-chief of the armed forces.

Given the gravity of this decision, it's crucial that we as voters approach this choice with the seriousness it deserves. This means moving beyond partisan loyalties and sound bites to engage deeply with the issues at hand. It means being willing to challenge our own assumptions and biases, to consider perspectives different from our own, and to base our decisions on facts rather than emotions.

In the chapters that follow, we will delve into fifteen key reasons why Kamala Harris presents a compelling choice for the presidency. We'll examine her stance on critical issues such as healthcare, education, climate change, and foreign policy. We'll look at her leadership style, her ability to build coalitions, and her vision for America's future. And we'll contrast these with Donald Trump's record and proposals, providing a clear picture of the choice before us.

Each chapter will provide a detailed analysis of a specific aspect of Harris's candidacy, supported by facts, quotes, and policy details. We'll examine her track record, her proposed policies, and expert opinions on their potential impacts. We'll also address criticisms and controversies, striving to present a balanced and honest assessment.

At the same time, we'll explore Trump's positions and record on these same issues, allowing for a direct comparison. This side-by-side analysis will help illustrate the stark differences between the two candidates and the potential consequences of choosing one over the other.

It's worth noting that no candidate is perfect, and no single book can capture every nuance of a presidential race. We encourage you to use this book as a starting point for your own research and reflection. Fact-check the information presented here, seek out additional sources, and engage in discussions with others who may have different perspectives.

Remember, the power of democracy lies in the hands of informed citizens. Your vote is your voice, and it matters. Whether you're a first-time voter or have been casting ballots for decades, whether you're firmly decided or still undecided, we hope this book will provide valuable insights to help you make an informed decision.

As we embark on this exploration of Kamala Harris's candidacy and the choice before us, let's commit to approaching this process with open minds, critical thinking, and a genuine desire to understand the issues at stake. Let's move beyond partisan rhetoric and superficial analysis to engage with the substantive differences between the candidates and their visions for America.

The challenges facing our nation are significant, but so too are the opportunities. We stand at a crossroads, with the power to shape the direction of our country for years to come. The decision we make will impact not just our own lives, but the lives of future generations.

So let us begin this journey of discovery, analysis, and informed decision-making. Let us examine the case for Kamala Harris with both scrutiny and an open mind. And let us approach this vital civic duty with the seriousness and thoughtfulness it deserves.

The future of our nation depends on it. The choice is in our hands.

Chapter 1:

Experience and Qualifications
The Foundation of Leadership

In the realm of presidential politics, few factors carry as much weight as a candidate's experience and qualifications. The role of President of the United States is arguably the most challenging and complex leadership position in the world, requiring a unique blend of skills, knowledge, and experience. As we embark on this critical evaluation of Kamala Harris's candidacy, it's essential to begin by examining her background in comparison to that of Donald Trump, and to understand why her extensive political experience and legal expertise make her a compelling choice for the presidency.

1. Harris's Extensive Political Experience

Kamala Harris's journey in public service spans over two decades, during which she has served in various roles at different levels of government. This diverse experience has given her a comprehensive understanding of how government works at local, state, and federal levels - a crucial asset for anyone aspiring to the highest office in the land.

Harris began her career in 1990 as a deputy district attorney in Alameda County, California. In this role, she prosecuted cases involving violent crimes, including homicide and child sexual assault. This early experience in the criminal justice system provided her with firsthand knowledge of the challenges and complexities of law enforcement and criminal prosecution. It also gave her valuable insights into the human impact of crime and the importance of both justice and compassion in the legal system.

In 2003, Harris took a significant step forward in her career when she was elected as the District Attorney of San Francisco. This victory was historic, as she became the first person of color to hold this position. During her tenure as District Attorney, Harris demonstrated her innovative approach to criminal justice by implementing programs aimed at reducing recidivism rates. One of her most notable initiatives was "Back on Track," a program that provided job training and other resources to first-time drug offenders. This program was so successful that it was later used as a model for reentry programs across the country, showcasing Harris's ability to develop effective, forward-thinking solutions to complex social problems.

Harris's next major career move came in 2010 when she was elected as the Attorney General of California. This position once again put her in the history books, as she became the first woman, first African American, and first South Asian American to hold this office. As Attorney General, Harris oversaw the second-largest justice department in the United States, second only to the U.S. Department of Justice. This role significantly expanded her responsibilities and provided her with invaluable experience in managing a large government organization and addressing complex legal and policy issues on a statewide scale.

During her time as Attorney General, Harris tackled a wide range of issues that affected the lives of millions of Californians. She took on cases involving consumer protection, fighting against predatory lending practices that had devastated many families during the financial crisis. She also focused on environmental regulation, working to ensure that corporations were held accountable for pollution and environmental damage. Civil rights were another key area of focus, with Harris using her office to advocate for marriage equality and against discrimination.

One of Harris's most significant achievements as Attorney General came in the wake of the 2008 financial crisis. She played a crucial role in securing a $20 billion settlement for California homeowners who had been affected by the foreclosure crisis. This accomplishment demonstrated her ability to stand up to powerful interests on behalf of ordinary citizens, a quality that many voters look for in a potential president.

In 2016, Harris's political career reached the national stage when she was elected to the United States Senate. As a Senator, she served on several key committees that provided her with crucial experience in national governance. Her position on the Select Committee on Intelligence gave her in-depth knowledge of national security matters and access to classified information about threats facing the nation. Her role on the Homeland Security and Governmental Affairs Committee provided her with insights into the workings of the federal government and issues related to national safety. Perhaps most notably, her position on the Judiciary Committee allowed her to play a key role in the confirmation processes for federal judges and high-ranking Justice Department officials, further deepening her understanding of the legal and constitutional issues facing the nation.

Harris's ascent to national prominence culminated in 2020 with her election as Vice President of the United States, making her the highest-ranking woman in the history of American government. In this role, she has been involved in high-level policy discussions, diplomatic engagements, and crisis management, further broadening her experience in executive leadership at the highest level of government. As Vice President, Harris has been tasked with leading on key administration priorities, including addressing the root causes of migration from Central America and expanding voting rights.

When we contrast this extensive political resume with Donald Trump's background, the differences are stark. Prior to becoming president in 2016, Trump had no experience in government or public service. His background was primarily in real estate development and reality television. While his supporters argued that his business experience was an asset, bringing a fresh perspective to Washington, critics pointed out that running a government is fundamentally different from running a business, requiring a different set of skills and knowledge.

Trump's lack of political experience was evident in several ways during his presidency. He often struggled with the intricacies of the legislative process, as seen in the failed attempt to repeal and replace the Affordable Care Act. His unconventional approach to diplomacy, while praised by some for its boldness, was criticized by others for damaging long-standing alliances and norms of international relations. Many of his policy initiatives faced legal challenges, with some, like early versions of the travel ban on several Muslim-majority countries, being struck down by the courts.

Harris's extensive political experience, spanning local, state, and federal government, provides her with a comprehensive understanding of how government works at all levels. This knowledge is crucial for effective governance, especially in a system as complex as the United States federal government. It allows her to navigate the intricacies of policy making, understand the potential impacts and unintended consequences of legislation, and work effectively with various branches and levels of government to achieve her goals.

2. Harris's Legal Expertise

Another significant advantage that Kamala Harris brings to the table is her legal expertise. As a graduate of Howard University and the University of California, Hastings College of the Law, Harris has a strong foundation in constitutional law and the American legal system. This background is particularly valuable for a president, who must navigate complex legal issues, make decisions that will withstand legal scrutiny, and nominate federal judges, including Supreme Court justices.

Harris's career as a prosecutor, District Attorney, and Attorney General has given her extensive experience in interpreting and applying the law. This practical legal experience is invaluable in understanding how laws impact real people and communities. It also provides her with insights into the challenges and limitations of the legal system, informing her approach to criminal justice reform and other legal issues.

During her time in the Senate, Harris's legal acumen was on full display, particularly during her questioning of Trump administration officials and judicial nominees in Senate hearings. Her sharp, incisive questioning often drew praise and demonstrated her ability to cut through obscurity and get to the heart of legal and constitutional issues. This skill is crucial for a president who must often make quick decisions on complex legal matters and communicate them effectively to the American people.

Harris's legal expertise is especially crucial in an era where many of the most pressing national issues have significant legal dimensions. From immigration reform and voting rights to privacy laws and regulatory policy, a deep understanding of the law is invaluable for a president seeking to implement effective policies that can withstand legal challenges.

Donald Trump, in contrast, does not have formal legal training. While he was involved in numerous lawsuits throughout his business career, this is not equivalent to the comprehensive legal knowledge that comes from legal education and practice. During his presidency, some of Trump's key policy initiatives faced significant legal challenges, highlighting the importance of a strong legal foundation for effective governance.

3. Harris's Understanding of Criminal Justice Issues

Given the ongoing national conversation about police reform and racial justice, Harris's background in law enforcement provides her with unique insights into these critical issues. While her record as a prosecutor has been a source of both praise and criticism, it undeniably gives her a nuanced understanding of the criminal justice system that few presidential candidates possess.

Harris has proposed comprehensive criminal justice reform plans, including ending private prisons, eliminating cash bail, and investing in rehabilitation and reentry programs. Her firsthand experience in the system allows her to approach these issues with a level of depth and nuance that is crucial for effective reform. She understands the complexities of the system, the perspectives of law enforcement, and the impacts on communities, particularly communities of color.

During her time as California's Attorney General, Harris implemented several reform initiatives. She created the first statewide implicit bias and procedural justice training for police officers, launched a database to increase transparency around in-custody deaths and police shootings, and established a body camera pilot program for state law enforcement officers. These efforts demonstrate her commitment to addressing systemic issues in law enforcement while also recognizing the important role that police play in maintaining public safety.

Trump, on the other hand, approached criminal justice issues primarily from a "law and order" perspective, often advocating for tougher sentencing and increased police powers. While he did sign the First Step Act, a bipartisan criminal justice reform bill, into law, his overall approach was generally seen as less reform-oriented than Harris's. Trump's lack of direct experience in the criminal justice system meant that his policies were often influenced more by political considerations than by a deep understanding of the system's complexities.

4. Harris's Diplomatic Experience

As Vice President and as a member of the Senate Intelligence Committee, Kamala Harris has gained significant experience in foreign policy and diplomacy. She has been involved in high-level diplomatic engagements, received classified intelligence briefings, and participated in crucial national security decisions. This experience is vital for a potential president, who must navigate complex international relationships, make critical decisions about military deployments, and represent the United States on the global stage.

Harris has demonstrated a nuanced understanding of global affairs, advocating for a return to multilateralism and the strengthening of traditional alliances. She has emphasized the importance of diplomacy in resolving international conflicts and addressing global challenges such as climate change and pandemic response. Her approach reflects a deep understanding of the interconnected nature of today's world and the need for cooperative international action to address many of the most pressing issues facing the nation.

During her time in the Senate, Harris served on the Intelligence Committee, which provided her with in-depth knowledge of national security threats and the workings of the intelligence community. This experience is crucial for a president, who must make difficult decisions based on complex and often ambiguous intelligence information.

As Vice President, Harris has been involved in several key diplomatic initiatives. She has held meetings with world leaders, represented the United States at international forums, and been tasked with leading on specific foreign policy issues, such as addressing the root causes of migration from Central America. These experiences have further honed her diplomatic skills and deepened her understanding of global affairs.

Trump's approach to foreign policy was characterized by his "America First" doctrine, which often put him at odds with traditional U.S. allies and international institutions. While supporters praised this as a bold new direction, critics argued that it damaged America's global standing and influence. Trump's unconventional approach to diplomacy, including his use of Twitter to communicate foreign policy decisions and his personal meetings with North Korean leader Kim Jong Un, was a significant departure from traditional diplomatic norms.

5. Harris's Crisis Management Experience

The COVID-19 pandemic has underscored the importance of effective crisis management skills in a president. As Vice President, Harris has been intimately involved in the federal government's response to the pandemic, giving her valuable experience in managing a national crisis. She has worked on efforts to accelerate vaccine distribution, support small businesses affected by the economic downturn, and address the pandemic's disproportionate impact on communities of color.

Moreover, her time as Attorney General of California involved managing the state's response to various crises, from natural disasters to public health emergencies. During her tenure, California faced severe droughts, wildfires, and the aftermath of the 2008 financial crisis. Harris's experience in crisis management at both the state and federal level is a significant asset for a potential president, demonstrating her ability to lead effectively under pressure and coordinate complex government responses to emergencies.

> My mother had a saying: 'Kamala, you may be the first to do many things, but make sure you're not the last.'
>
> **Kamala Harris**

Trump's handling of the COVID-19 pandemic was a major point of contention during his presidency. Critics argued that his initial downplaying of the virus's severity and his conflicts with public health officials hampered the nation's response. While defenders pointed to his early travel restrictions and efforts to accelerate vaccine development, the overall U.S. response to the pandemic under Trump's leadership was widely criticized by public health experts.

6. Harris's Collaborative Leadership Style

Throughout her career, Kamala Harris has demonstrated an ability to work across the aisle and build coalitions to achieve policy goals. As Attorney General, she worked with both Democrats and Republicans in the California legislature to pass important legislation. In the Senate, she co-sponsored bills with Republican colleagues on issues such as election security and apprenticeship programs.

This collaborative approach is crucial in today's polarized political environment. A president must be able to build consensus and work with Congress to pass legislation and implement policies. Harris's track record suggests she has the skills to navigate these challenges effectively. Her ability to find common ground with political opponents while still standing firm on her core principles is a valuable asset in a leader.

Trump's leadership style, by contrast, was often confrontational and divisive. While this energized his base, it also made it difficult to build the broad coalitions often necessary for major policy achievements. His frequent use of Twitter to attack political opponents and his tendency to label critics as "enemies" contributed to a highly polarized political climate.

7. Harris's Commitment to Public Service

Finally, it's worth noting that Kamala Harris's entire career has been dedicated to public service. From her early days as a prosecutor to her current role as Vice President, Harris has consistently chosen to work in the public sector, demonstrating a commitment to serving the American people.

This dedication to public service suggests a genuine desire to work for the common good and improve the lives of all Americans. It stands in contrast to Trump's background in private business, where the primary goal is typically profit rather than public benefit. While business acumen can certainly be valuable in governance, Harris's career-long focus on public service indicates a deep-seated commitment to the principles of democracy and the responsibilities of government.

Throughout her career, Harris has often spoken about her motivations for entering public service, frequently citing her parents' involvement in the civil rights movement and her desire to be a voice for the voiceless. This sense of purpose and commitment to public service is an important quality in a potential president, as it suggests a leader who will prioritize the needs of the nation over personal or political gain.

Conclusion

When we examine the experience and qualifications of Kamala Harris and Donald Trump, we see two very different profiles. Harris brings to the table extensive experience in government at multiple levels, deep legal expertise, a nuanced understanding of criminal justice issues, diplomatic experience, crisis management skills, a collaborative leadership style, and a career-long commitment to public service.

Trump, on the other hand, came to the presidency with a background in business and entertainment, but no prior experience in government or public service. While his supporters argued that his outsider status was an asset, bringing a fresh perspective to Washington, his presidency demonstrated the challenges that can arise from a lack of political experience and wisdom that comes with experience.

In an increasingly complex world, with challenges ranging from climate change and economic inequality to global pandemics and geopolitical tensions, the value of Harris's diverse and relevant experience cannot be overstated. Her background has prepared her to navigate the intricacies of government, understand and address complex policy issues, work collaboratively with diverse stakeholders, and represent America effectively on the world stage.

Harris's legal background provides her with a strong foundation for understanding and addressing the complex legal issues that often arise in governance. Her experience in law enforcement and criminal justice gives her unique insights into one of the most pressing issues facing the nation today. Her diplomatic experience and crisis management skills are crucial assets in an era of global challenges and unexpected crises.

Moreover, Harris's collaborative leadership style and commitment to public service suggest a leader who can work to heal the divisions in our society and restore faith in government institutions. Her ability to build coalitions and find common ground, even in a polarized political environment, is a crucial skill for effective governance.

Of course, experience and qualifications are not the only factors to consider when choosing a president. Policy positions, character, vision for the country, and many other elements all play important roles. However, when it comes to the crucial aspect of being prepared for the immense responsibilities of the presidency, Kamala Harris's extensive and relevant experience makes her a compelling choice.

As we continue to explore the case for Kamala Harris in the following chapters, we'll delve deeper into her policy proposals, leadership style, and vision for America's future. But this foundation of experience and qualifications provides a strong starting point for her candidacy, offering voters the assurance that she is well-prepared for the challenges of the presidency.

In a time of great national and global challenges, the value of experienced, knowledgeable leadership cannot be overstated. Kamala Harris's background in law, governance, and public service positions her uniquely well to take on the immense responsibilities of the presidency and to lead America forward into an uncertain future.

Chapter 2

Leadership Style and Character
The Essence of Presidential Mettle

When evaluating presidential candidates, their leadership style and character are paramount considerations. These qualities shape how a president will govern, interact with allies and adversaries, and navigate the complex challenges of the office. In this chapter, we'll examine Kamala Harris's leadership style and character in comparison to Donald Trump's, highlighting why Harris's approach may be better suited for the challenges facing America today.

1. Collaborative vs. Confrontational Leadership

Kamala Harris has consistently demonstrated a collaborative leadership style throughout her career. This approach is characterized by her ability to work across party lines, build coalitions, and find common ground on complex issues. During her time as California's Attorney General and later as a U.S. Senator, Harris frequently reached across the aisle to work with Republicans on various initiatives.

For instance, as Attorney General, Harris worked with both Democratic and Republican state legislators to pass the California Homeowner Bill of Rights in 2012. This landmark legislation provided protections for homeowners facing foreclosure and was widely praised as a bipartisan achievement. In the Senate, Harris co-sponsored bills with Republican colleagues on issues such as election security and apprenticeship programs, showcasing her ability to find areas of agreement even in a highly polarized political environment.

Harris's collaborative approach extends beyond just working with political opponents. She has a track record of engaging with diverse stakeholders, including community leaders, advocacy groups, and experts in various fields, to develop comprehensive solutions to complex problems. This inclusive style of leadership allows for a broader range of perspectives to be considered in policymaking, potentially leading to more effective and widely accepted solutions.

In contrast, Donald Trump's leadership style has been characterized as confrontational and divisive. Throughout his presidency, Trump often used inflammatory rhetoric against political opponents, the media, and even members of his own party who disagreed with him. His frequent use of Social Media to attack critics and make policy announcements often caught even his own administration off guard, leading to confusion and sometimes contradicting official White House positions.

Trump's "my way or the highway" approach to leadership often made it difficult to build the broad coalitions necessary for significant policy achievements. While his base strongly supported this style, viewing it as a refreshing departure from traditional politics, critics argued that it deepened political divisions and made compromise more difficult. Unable to get policy through congress he resorted to Executive Orders 220 times.

The implications of these differing leadership styles are significant. In an era of intense political polarization, a president's ability to bridge divides and build consensus is crucial. Harris's collaborative approach suggests she may be better equipped to navigate the complex political landscape and achieve meaningful progress on key issues. Her style aligns more closely with the traditional view of the president as a unifying figure who can bring the country together in times of crisis or division.

2. Empathy and Emotional Intelligence

Another critical aspect of leadership is emotional intelligence, including the ability to empathize with others and manage one's own emotions effectively. Kamala Harris has frequently demonstrated these qualities throughout her career.

Harris's background as the daughter of immigrants and her experience as a woman of color in high-profile leadership positions have informed her ability to empathize with a wide range of Americans. She often speaks about the struggles of working families, the challenges faced by minorities, and the importance of creating opportunities for all Americans. This empathy is not just rhetorical; it has informed her policy positions on issues ranging from healthcare and education to criminal justice reform.

During her time as a prosecutor and Attorney General, Harris implemented programs that showed a nuanced understanding of the human factors involved in crime and rehabilitation. For example, her "Back on Track" program for first-time drug offenders focused on education and job training rather than purely punitive measures, demonstrating an empathetic approach to criminal justice.

As a Senator and Vice President, Harris has been known for her ability to connect with people on a personal level during public events and town halls. She listens attentively to constituents' concerns and often shares personal anecdotes that relate to their experiences, showing an ability to understand and validate others' perspectives.

Donald Trump, on the other hand, has been criticized for a perceived lack of empathy in various situations. His response to natural disasters, such as Hurricane Maria in Puerto Rico, was seen by many as inadequate and lacking in compassion. His rhetoric on sensitive issues like immigration and racial justice often seemed to dismiss or minimize the concerns and experiences of marginalized communities. In times of national crisis or tragedy, many Americans looked for a more empathetic and unifying voice from their leader.

The ability to empathize and demonstrate emotional intelligence is crucial for a president. It allows a leader to understand and respond effectively to the needs and concerns of diverse constituencies, to navigate delicate diplomatic situations, and to provide comfort and leadership during times of national crisis. Harris's demonstrated capacity for empathy suggests she may be better equipped to fulfill this aspect of presidential leadership.

3. Adaptability and Willingness to Learn

In an era of rapid technological change and evolving global challenges, a president's ability to adapt and learn is crucial. Kamala Harris has shown a consistent willingness to evolve her positions and approach based on new information and changing circumstances.

Throughout her career, Harris has demonstrated an ability to listen to criticism and adjust her stance on various issues. For example, her views on criminal justice reform have evolved over time, moving from a more traditional "tough on crime" approach early in her career as a prosecutor to embracing more progressive reforms as Attorney General and Senator. This evolution shows a willingness to reassess long-held positions in light of new evidence and changing societal attitudes.

> Here's the thing: every office I've run for I was the first to win. First person of color. First woman. First woman of color. Every time.
> Kamala Harris

Harris has also shown an eagerness to engage with experts and learn about complex issues. During her time in the Senate, she was known for her thorough preparation and insightful questioning during committee hearings, often delving into technical details on a wide range of topics from cybersecurity to climate science.

Donald Trump, in contrast, often prided himself on trusting his instincts over expert advice. He frequently dismissed or contradicted his own administration's experts, most notably during the COVID-19 pandemic when he publicly disagreed with public health officials on the severity of the virus and the effectiveness of measures like mask-wearing.

Trump's approach was often characterized as valuing decisiveness over technical expertise. While this resonated with supporters who felt that traditional politicians were out of touch with ordinary Americans, it also led to criticism that complex policy decisions were being made without sufficient understanding of their implications and without considering sound advice from his staff.

In a rapidly changing world, a president's willingness to adapt, learn, and incorporate expert knowledge into decision-making is crucial. Harris's demonstrated ability to evolve her positions and engage deeply with complex issues suggests she may be better prepared to tackle the multifaceted challenges facing the nation.

4. Integrity and Transparency

The fundamental qualities of integrity and transparency are essential traits for maintaining public trust in government institutions and ensuring accountability in the highest office of the land.

Throughout her career, Kamala Harris has maintained a reputation for integrity. As a prosecutor and Attorney General, she was known for her ethical approach to law enforcement and her efforts to increase transparency in the criminal justice system. For example, she implemented a database to increase transparency around in-custody deaths and police shootings in California.

As a Senator, Harris was an advocate for government transparency, supporting legislation to make congressional reports more accessible to the public and pushing for greater disclosure of political advertising on social media platforms. She has also been consistent in releasing her tax returns, a practice she continued as a vice-presidential and presidential candidate.

Donald Trump's presidency, on the other hand, was marked by numerous controversies related to integrity and transparency. His refusal to release his tax returns broke with decades of presidential tradition and raised questions about potential conflicts of interest. The numerous ethics investigations into members of his administration, including several cabinet secretaries who resigned due to scandals, also raised concerns about the overall integrity of his government.

Trump's frequent clashes with the press, including his labeling of unfavorable coverage as "fake news," were seen by many as an attempt to undermine the media's role in ensuring government accountability. His administration's resistance to congressional oversight, including in the impeachment proceedings, also raised concerns about transparency and the separation of powers.

While Trump's supporters often viewed these issues as evidence of his willingness to challenge the political establishment, critics saw them as threats to democratic norms and institutions. The contrast between Harris's record of advocating for transparency and Trump's more opaque approach highlights a significant difference in their approach to governance.

5. Crisis Management and Decision-Making

A president's ability to manage crises and make sound decisions under pressure is perhaps one of the most critical aspects of the job. Kamala Harris's experience in executive roles, particularly as Attorney General of California and as Vice President, has given her valuable experience in crisis management.

As California's Attorney General, Harris had to respond to various crises, including natural disasters, public health emergencies, and the aftermath of the 2008 financial crisis. Her handling of these situations demonstrated an ability to coordinate complex government responses and communicate effectively with the public during challenging times.

As Vice President, Harris has been involved in managing some of the most significant crises facing the nation, including the ongoing COVID-19 pandemic and its economic fallout. Her approach has typically involved relying on expert advice, coordinating across various government agencies, and emphasizing clear, consistent public communication.

Donald Trump's crisis management style, particularly evident during the COVID-19 pandemic, was markedly different. His approach was often characterized by downplaying the severity of the crisis, contradicting public health experts, and prioritizing economic concerns over public health measures. While supporters praised his optimism and focus on the economy, critics argued that this approach hampered the effectiveness of the nation's response to the pandemic.

Trump's decision-making process was often described as intuitive and based on personal relationships rather than formal processes. This was evident in his frequent policy announcements via Twitter, sometimes catching his own administration off guard. While this unconventional style was praised by supporters as nimble and direct, critics argued it led to confusion and inconsistency in policy implementation.

The contrasting approaches to crisis management and decision-making between Harris and Trump highlight significant differences in leadership style. Harris's more methodical, expert-driven approach aligns more closely with traditional expectations of presidential leadership, particularly in times of crisis.

6. Commitment to Democratic Norms and Institutions

A crucial aspect of presidential leadership in a democracy is a commitment to upholding democratic norms and institutions. This includes respecting the separation of powers, defending the independence of the judiciary and the press, and ensuring the integrity of elections.

Throughout her career, Kamala Harris has consistently demonstrated a strong commitment to these democratic principles. As a Senator, she was a vocal defender of the independence of the Justice Department and the FBI, particularly during the Russia investigation. She has also been a strong advocate for voting rights, sponsoring legislation to strengthen election security and combat voter suppression.

Harris's rhetoric consistently emphasizes the importance of democratic institutions and the rule of law. She frequently speaks about the need to protect and strengthen American democracy, framing many policy issues within this context.

Donald Trump's presidency, in contrast, was marked by numerous controversies related to democratic norms and institutions. His frequent attacks on the media as the "enemy of the people," his criticism of judges who ruled against his policies, and his attempts to influence Justice Department investigations were seen by many as threats to the norms that underpin American democracy.

The events surrounding the 2020 election, including Trump's unfounded claims of widespread voter fraud and the January 6th Capitol riot, raised serious concerns about his commitment to the peaceful transfer of power - a cornerstone of democratic governance.

While Trump's supporters often viewed his actions as necessary to "drain the swamp" and challenge a corrupt establishment, critics saw them as dangerous erosions of democratic norms and institutions. The stark contrast between Harris's consistent support for democratic principles and Trump's more combative approach to these institutions represents a fundamental difference in their vision of presidential leadership.

7. Representation and Inclusivity

In an increasingly diverse nation, a president's ability to represent and include all Americans is more important than ever. Kamala Harris's background as the daughter of immigrants, a woman of color, and the first female Vice President positions her uniquely to understand and represent a wide range of American experiences.

Throughout her career, Harris has been a vocal advocate for inclusivity and diversity. She has consistently pushed for policies that address racial and gender disparities, from her work on maternal mortality rates among Black women to her advocacy for LGBTQ+ rights. Her presence in leadership roles has itself been a powerful symbol of progress and representation for many Americans.

Harris's approach to policy making often involves seeking input from diverse communities and considering the impact of policies on different demographic groups. This inclusive approach to governance suggests a leadership style that aims to represent and serve all Americans.

Donald Trump's approach to representation and inclusivity was markedly different. His rhetoric often alienated minority communities, from his comments about Mexican immigrants during his campaign launch to his handling of racial justice protests during his presidency. While Trump and his supporters argued that his policies, such as low unemployment rates for minority communities, spoke louder than his rhetoric, many saw his approach as divisive and exclusionary.

Trump's administration was also noted for its lack of diversity, particularly in high-level positions. This stood in stark contrast to previous administrations of both parties, which had made concerted efforts to ensure diverse representation in government.

The difference in approach to representation and inclusivity between Harris and Trump reflects fundamentally different visions of American society and the role of the presidency. Harris's inclusive approach and her own groundbreaking role suggest a leadership style more attuned to the diverse experiences and needs of all Americans.

Conclusion

As we examine the leadership styles and character of Kamala Harris and Donald Trump, we see two markedly different approaches to the presidency. Harris's collaborative, empathetic, and inclusive leadership style stands in stark contrast to Trump's more confrontational and divisive approach.

Harris's demonstrated ability to work across party lines, her empathy and emotional intelligence, her adaptability and willingness to learn, her commitment to integrity and transparency, her methodical approach to crisis management, her strong support for democratic norms and institutions, and her emphasis on representation and inclusivity all suggest a leadership style well-suited to the challenges facing America today.

Her collaborative approach could be particularly valuable in addressing the deep political divisions that currently characterize American politics. Her empathy and emotional intelligence could help in healing national wounds and providing comfort during times of crisis. Her adaptability and willingness to learn are crucial traits in an era of rapid technological change and evolving global challenges.

Harris's commitment to integrity and transparency could help restore faith in government institutions, while her methodical approach to crisis management could provide stability and confidence in turbulent times. Her strong support for democratic norms and institutions is particularly relevant given recent challenges to these foundations of American democracy. Finally, her emphasis on representation and inclusivity could help in addressing long-standing inequities and ensuring that government truly serves all Americans.

Donald Trump's presidency, while praised by supporters for its boldness and willingness to challenge the status quo, raised significant concerns about the erosion of democratic norms, the deepening of political divisions, and the undermining of America's global leadership role. His confrontational style, while energizing to his base, often made it difficult to build the broad coalitions necessary for significant policy achievements.

As we look to the future, the choice between these leadership styles is not just about policy positions or political ideology. It's about the very nature of the presidency itself - how the office should function, what it should represent, and how it can best serve the American people in these challenging times.

Kamala Harris's leadership style and character, as demonstrated throughout her career, align more closely with traditional expectations of presidential leadership. Her approach suggests a presidency that would seek to unite rather than divide, to build rather than tear down, and to lead with empathy, integrity, and a commitment to democratic values.

In an era of intense political polarization, global uncertainty, and domestic challenges, Harris's leadership style could provide a steadying influence and a path towards addressing the nation's problems through collaboration, inclusivity, and a respect for democratic institutions. As we continue to make the case for Kamala Harris in the following chapters, this foundation of leadership and character provides a compelling argument for her fitness for the highest office in the land.

Chapter 3

Domestic Policy
Shaping America's Future at Home

The domestic policies of a president have a profound impact on the daily lives of Americans, shaping everything from healthcare and education to economic opportunity and social justice. In this chapter, we'll examine Kamala Harris's approach to key domestic issues, contrasting her positions with those of Donald Trump, and explore why her vision may be better suited to address the challenges facing America today.

1. Healthcare: Expanding Access and Affordability

Healthcare remains one of the most pressing issues for Americans, with concerns about access, affordability, and quality at the forefront of national debate. Kamala Harris has been a strong advocate for expanding healthcare access and affordability throughout her career.

As a Senator, Harris was a co-sponsor of Bernie Sanders' Medicare for All bill, which aimed to create a single-payer healthcare system. However, recognizing the political challenges of implementing such a sweeping change, Harris later developed her own healthcare plan. This plan proposes a system that would provide universal coverage through a expanded Medicare system, while also allowing private insurers to offer plans that comply with Medicare requirements.

Key elements of Harris's healthcare vision include:

- Automatic enrollment of all Americans in an expanded Medicare system
- A 10-year phase-in period to smooth the transition
- Allowance for private insurers to offer Medicare plans that meet strict requirements
- Cap on out-of-pocket costs for consumers
- Expanded coverage for mental health services and addiction treatment
- Measures to lower prescription drug prices, including allowing Medicare to negotiate drug prices

Harris argues that this approach would achieve universal coverage while providing more choice than a pure single-payer system. She also emphasizes the importance of addressing racial disparities in healthcare outcomes, proposing increased funding for research into diseases that disproportionately affect minorities and measures to address maternal mortality rates among women of color.

In contrast, Donald Trump's healthcare policy focused primarily on dismantling the Affordable Care Act (ACA), also known as Obamacare. While his administration was unable to fully repeal the ACA, it did take steps to weaken it, including eliminating the individual mandate penalty and expanding access to less comprehensive, short-term health plans.

Trump promised to replace the ACA with a better healthcare plan, but his administration never put forward a comprehensive alternative. His approach emphasized market-based solutions and state flexibility, arguing that this would lead to lower costs and more choice for consumers.

The contrast between Harris and Trump on healthcare is stark. While Harris seeks to expand government's role in ensuring universal coverage, Trump advocated for reducing government involvement and relying more heavily on market forces. Harris's approach aligns more closely with the majority of Americans who, according to polls, believe the government should play a significant role in ensuring healthcare access for all citizens.

2. Economic Policy: Building a More Equitable Economy

Economic policy is another area where Kamala Harris and Donald Trump offer markedly different visions for America's future. Harris's economic policies focus on addressing income inequality, supporting the middle class, and creating opportunities for disadvantaged communities.

Key elements of Harris's economic vision include:

- Raising the minimum wage to $15 per hour
- Implementing a $3 trillion tax plan that would increase taxes on corporations and the wealthy while providing tax credits for lower- and middle-income Americans
- Investing in infrastructure and clean energy to create jobs
- Strengthening workers' rights, including support for unions and paid family leave
- Addressing the racial wealth gap through measures such as investment in historically black colleges and universities (HBCUs) and support for minority-owned businesses

Harris has also proposed a signature policy called the LIFT (Livable Incomes for Families Today) Act, which would provide a refundable tax credit of up to $6,000 a year for families earning less than $100,000 annually. This policy aims to provide immediate financial relief to struggling families and boost economic growth by increasing consumer spending.

> *I always start my campaigns early, and I run hard. Maybe it comes from the rough-and-tumble world of San Francisco politics, where it's not even a contact sport - it's a blood sport. This is how I am as a candidate. This is how I run campaigns.*
> **Kamala Harris**

Donald Trump's economic policies, on the other hand, centered around tax cuts and deregulation. The cornerstone of his economic agenda was the 2017 Tax Cuts and Jobs Act, which significantly reduced corporate tax rates and provided tax cuts across all income brackets, with the largest benefits going to high-income earners and corporations.

Trump argued that these tax cuts, combined with his administration's efforts to roll back regulations on businesses, would stimulate economic growth and job creation. His supporters point to the strong pre-pandemic economy, with low unemployment rates and a booming stock market, as evidence of the success of these policies.

Critics, however, argue that Trump's economic policies exacerbated income inequality and disproportionately benefited the wealthy and large corporations. They also point out that the long-term effects of the tax cuts on the national debt raise concerns about fiscal sustainability.

The contrast between Harris and Trump on economic policy reflects fundamentally different philosophies about how to create prosperity. While Trump's approach relied heavily on the theory of "trickle-down" economics, Harris's policies aim to build the economy "from the middle out and the bottom up." Her focus on addressing income inequality and providing direct support to lower- and middle-income Americans aligns with growing concerns about economic disparities in the United States.

3. Criminal Justice Reform: Addressing Systemic Inequities

Criminal justice reform has become a major issue in American politics, particularly in light of high-profile incidents of police brutality and racial disparities in the justice system. Kamala Harris's background as a prosecutor and Attorney General gives her a unique perspective on this issue, and her views have evolved significantly over the course of her career.

As a presidential candidate and Vice President, Harris has advocated for comprehensive criminal justice reform. Key elements of her vision include:

- Ending mandatory minimum sentences for non-violent drug offenses
- Abolishing the death penalty at the federal level
- Ending cash bail, which disproportionately affects low-income individuals
- Investing in rehabilitation and reentry programs to reduce recidivism
- Legalizing marijuana at the federal level and expunging past convictions

- Implementing national standards for police use of force and increasing accountability measures

Harris has also been a strong advocate for addressing racial disparities in the criminal justice system. She supports measures to combat racial profiling, reform sentencing guidelines that have disproportionately affected minorities, and increase diversity in law enforcement and the judiciary.

Donald Trump's approach to criminal justice was characterized by his "law and order" rhetoric. He advocated for tougher sentences for violent offenders and took a hard line on issues like immigration enforcement. However, he did sign the First Step Act, a bipartisan criminal justice reform bill that reduced sentences for some federal offenses and expanded rehabilitation programs.

Trump's rhetoric on policing, particularly in response to the Black Lives Matter protests of 2020, was often seen as divisive. He strongly opposed calls to "defund the police" and criticized protesters, arguing that their actions were undermining law and order.

The contrast between Harris and Trump on criminal justice reform is significant. While Trump emphasized a more traditional "tough on crime" approach, Harris's policies reflect a growing consensus among criminal justice experts about the need for a more rehabilitative and equitable approach to law enforcement and incarceration.

Harris's evolution on this issue - from a prosecutor who at times took hardline positions to an advocate for comprehensive reform - may actually be an asset. It suggests an ability to learn from experience and adapt policies based on evidence and changing societal attitudes.

4. Education: Investing in America's Future

Education is another crucial area of domestic policy where Kamala Harris and Donald Trump offer contrasting visions. Harris sees education as a key tool for addressing inequality and preparing Americans for the jobs of the future.

Key elements of Harris's education policy include:

- Making community college free for all Americans
- Increasing teacher pay by an average of $13,500
- Expanding access to early childhood education
- Increasing federal funding for K-12 education, particularly in low-income areas
- Supporting debt-free college for students from families earning less than $125,000 per year
- Investing in HBCUs and other minority-serving institutions

Harris has also emphasized the importance of addressing the "homework gap" - the disparity in access to high-speed internet and digital devices that affects many low-income and rural students. She supports significant investment in broadband infrastructure to ensure all students have the tools they need to succeed in the digital age.

Donald Trump's education policies focused primarily on expanding school choice through measures like charter schools and voucher programs. His administration also rolled back several Obama-era education policies, including guidance on racial diversity in college admissions and protections for transgender students.

Trump's approach emphasized local control of education and reducing the federal government's role. He was a strong critic of teachers' unions and advocated for performance-based pay for teachers.

The contrast between Harris and Trump on education reflects different philosophies about the role of government in ensuring educational opportunity. While Trump emphasized market-based solutions and local control, Harris advocates for a more active federal role in addressing educational inequities and ensuring access to quality education at all levels.

5. Climate Change and Environmental Policy: Addressing the Global Crisis

Climate change is perhaps the most pressing long-term challenge facing not just the United States, but the entire world. Kamala Harris has made addressing climate change a key priority of her policy agenda.

Key elements of Harris's climate and environmental policies include:

- Achieving net-zero emissions by 2050
- Investing $10 trillion in clean energy and infrastructure over 10 years
- Implementing a carbon tax
- Rejoining the Paris Climate Agreement
- Ending fossil fuel subsidies and banning new fossil fuel leases on public lands
- Investing in climate resilience and adaptation measures, particularly for vulnerable communities

Harris frames climate change not just as an environmental issue, but as an economic opportunity. She argues that investments in clean energy and green infrastructure can create millions of well-paying jobs while also addressing the climate crisis.

Donald Trump, in contrast, was skeptical of climate change and pursued policies that prioritized fossil fuel production and rolled back environmental regulations. Key aspects of Trump's environmental policy included:

- Withdrawing from the Paris Climate Agreement
- Rolling back Obama-era emissions standards for vehicles
- Promoting coal, oil, and natural gas production
- Reducing the size of national monuments to allow for more resource extraction
- Weakening the Endangered Species Act

Trump argued that environmental regulations were hurting American businesses and workers, particularly in industries like coal mining. He framed his policies as protecting American jobs and energy independence.

The contrast between Harris and Trump on climate and environmental policy could not be starker. While Trump questioned the science of climate change and prioritized short-term economic considerations, Harris sees addressing climate change as both an environmental imperative and an economic opportunity. Her approach aligns more closely with the scientific consensus on the urgency of addressing climate change and the growing public concern about this issue.

6. Immigration: Balancing Security and Compassion

Immigration has been one of the most contentious issues in American politics in recent years. Kamala Harris's approach to immigration emphasizes both border security and a path to citizenship for undocumented immigrants, particularly those brought to the country as children.

Key elements of Harris's immigration policy include:

- Providing a path to citizenship for the approximately 11 million undocumented immigrants in the U.S.
- Protecting DACA (Deferred Action for Childhood Arrivals) recipients and their families
- Implementing smarter border security measures, focusing on technology rather than physical barriers
- Addressing the root causes of migration from Central America through aid and diplomatic efforts
- Reforming the legal immigration system to reduce backlogs and reunite families

Harris has been a vocal critic of Trump's immigration policies, particularly the separation of families at the border and the travel ban on several Muslim-majority countries.

Donald Trump made immigration a centerpiece of his political identity, campaigning on promises to build a wall on the U.S.-Mexico border and taking a hard line on both legal and illegal immigration. Key aspects of Trump's immigration policy included:

- Attempting to build a wall along the southern border

- Implementing a "zero tolerance" policy that led to family separations
- Imposing travel bans on several predominantly Muslim countries
- Reducing refugee admissions to historic lows
- Attempting to end the DACA program

Trump argued that these measures were necessary for national security and to protect American jobs. His supporters praised his tough stance on illegal immigration, while critics argued that his policies were inhumane and contrary to American values.

The contrast between Harris and Trump on immigration reflects fundamentally different views on America's role as a nation of immigrants. While Trump emphasized restriction and enforcement, Harris's approach seeks to balance security concerns with America's tradition of welcoming immigrants and the economic benefits of immigration.

7. Gun Control: Addressing America's Epidemic of Gun Violence

Gun violence remains a pressing issue in the United States, with mass shootings and everyday gun deaths continuing to shock the nation. Kamala Harris has been a strong advocate for gun control measures throughout her career.

Key elements of Harris's gun control policy include:

- Implementing universal background checks
- Banning assault weapons and high-capacity magazines

- Closing the "boyfriend loophole" to prevent domestic abusers from purchasing firearms
- Repealing the Protection of Lawful Commerce in Arms Act, which shields gun manufacturers from certain lawsuits
- Implementing a federal gun licensing program

Harris argues that these measures are necessary to address the epidemic of gun violence in America while respecting the Second Amendment rights of law-abiding citizens.

Donald Trump, backed by the National Rifle Association, took a strong pro-gun rights stance during his presidency. While he did ban bump stocks following the Las Vegas mass shooting, he generally opposed new gun control measures. Trump argued that the focus should be on mental health and school security rather than gun restrictions.

The contrast between Harris and Trump on gun control is significant. While Trump emphasized protecting gun ownership rights, Harris advocates for what she calls "reasonable" gun control measures to address gun violence. Her position aligns more closely with public opinion polls that show majority support for measures like universal background checks.

Conclusion

As we examine the domestic policy positions of Kamala Harris and Donald Trump, we see two fundamentally different visions for America's future. Harris's policies generally reflect a more active role for government in addressing societal challenges, from healthcare and economic inequality to climate change and gun violence. Her approach emphasizes equity, inclusivity, and long-term sustainability.

Trump's policies, on the other hand, tended to emphasize reduced government regulation, market-based solutions, and a more traditional approach to issues like criminal justice and immigration. His supporters argue that this approach led to economic growth and job creation, while critics contend that it exacerbated inequalities and ignored long-term challenges like climate change.

Harris's policy agenda is ambitious and would represent a significant shift in many areas of domestic policy. Her healthcare proposals aim to achieve universal coverage, her economic policies seek to address growing income inequality, her approach to criminal justice emphasizes reform and equity, her education policies focus on expanding access and addressing disparities, her climate policies align with the urgency expressed by scientists, her immigration policies balance security with compassion, and her gun control measures aim to address America's unique challenge with gun violence.

Critics may argue that Harris's proposals are too costly or represent too much government intervention. However, supporters would contend that bold action is necessary to address the significant challenges facing the nation, from healthcare access and income inequality to climate change and systemic racism.

As we continue to make the case for Kamala Harris, her domestic policy agenda represents a comprehensive and progressive vision for addressing America's challenges. While the feasibility of implementing all of these policies would depend on factors like

Congressional support, they provide a clear roadmap for the direction in which Harris would seek to lead the country.

In an era of growing inequality, ongoing racial tensions, and existential threats like climate change, Harris's policy agenda offers a path towards a more equitable, sustainable, and inclusive America. As voters consider their choice for president, these domestic policy positions provide a stark contrast and a clear choice for the future direction of the country.

Chapter 4

Economic Policy
Building a More Prosperous and Equitable America

The economic policies of a president have far-reaching consequences, affecting everything from job creation and wage growth to income inequality and the overall health of the nation's economy. In this chapter, we'll delve deeper into Kamala Harris's economic vision, comparing it with Donald Trump's approach, and explore why her policies may be better suited to address the economic challenges facing America today.

1. Tax Policy: Balancing Growth and Fairness

At the heart of any economic policy is the tax system, which not only generates revenue for government programs but also plays a crucial role in shaping economic incentives and addressing income inequality. Kamala Harris has proposed a comprehensive tax plan that aims to make the system more progressive while generating revenue for her policy priorities.

Key elements of Harris's tax plan include:

- Repealing portions of the 2017 Tax Cuts and Jobs Act that benefited corporations and high-income individuals
- Imposing a financial transaction tax on stock and bond trades

- Implementing a "millionaire's surtax" of 4% on incomes above $1 million
- Expanding the Earned Income Tax Credit (EITC) and Child Tax Credit
- Eliminating the stepped-up basis loophole that allows heirs to avoid capital gains taxes on inherited assets

Harris argues that these changes would make the tax system fairer while generating revenue for investments in healthcare, education, and infrastructure. She emphasizes that her tax increases would only affect the wealthiest Americans and corporations, with no tax increases for households making less than $400,000 a year.

In contrast, Donald Trump's signature economic policy was the 2017 Tax Cuts and Jobs Act. This legislation significantly reduced corporate tax rates from 35% to 21% and provided tax cuts across all income brackets, with the largest benefits going to high-income earners and corporations. Trump argued that these tax cuts would stimulate economic growth, job creation, and wage increases through a "trickle-down" effect.

The contrast between Harris and Trump on tax policy reflects fundamentally different philosophies about how to stimulate economic growth and address income inequality. While Trump's approach relied heavily on tax cuts for corporations and high-income individuals, Harris's plan seeks to make the tax system more progressive and generate revenue for social investments.

Critics of Harris's plan argue that higher taxes on corporations and the wealthy could stifle investment and job creation. However, proponents point out that similar tax rates in the past have coincided with strong economic growth, and that the revenue generated could fund investments in education, infrastructure, and healthcare that could boost long-term economic productivity.

2. Job Creation and Workforce Development

Creating good-paying jobs and preparing the American workforce for the challenges of the 21st century economy are crucial goals for any economic policy. Kamala Harris has proposed a multi-faceted approach to job creation and workforce development.

Key elements of Harris's jobs and workforce plan include:

- Investing $10 trillion in clean energy and infrastructure, which she argues would create millions of new jobs
- Implementing a $15 federal minimum wage
- Strengthening workers' rights, including making it easier for workers to unionize
- Investing in apprenticeship programs and vocational training
- Providing support for small businesses, particularly those owned by women and minorities
- Addressing the "care economy" by investing in childcare and eldercare jobs

Harris emphasizes the need to create "good-paying, union jobs" and to ensure that workers have the skills needed for the jobs of the future. She also focuses on addressing racial and gender disparities in employment and wages.

Donald Trump's approach to job creation centered around tax cuts, deregulation, and trade policy. He argued that lowering corporate tax rates and reducing regulations would encourage businesses to hire more workers and increase wages. Trump also emphasized bringing manufacturing jobs back to the United States through renegotiated trade deals and tariffs on imports.

While the pre-pandemic economy under Trump saw low unemployment rates, critics argue that many of the jobs created were low-wage positions and that wage growth was not as strong as the topline numbers suggested. They also point out that the manufacturing renaissance Trump promised did not fully materialize.

The contrast between Harris and Trump on job creation and workforce development is significant. While Trump relied primarily on tax cuts and deregulation to stimulate job growth, Harris proposes more direct government investment in job creation, particularly in emerging sectors like clean energy. Her focus on workers' rights and addressing disparities also represents a different approach to ensuring that economic growth benefits all Americans.

3. Trade Policy: Balancing Global Engagement and American Interests

In an increasingly interconnected global economy, trade policy plays a crucial role in shaping economic outcomes. Kamala Harris's approach to trade seeks to balance the benefits of global engagement with protections for American workers and environmental standards.

Key elements of Harris's trade policy include:

- Enforcing labor and environmental standards in trade agreements
- Addressing currency manipulation by trading partners

- Strengthening "Buy American" provisions in government procurement
- Investing in American manufacturing and innovation to enhance competitiveness
- Engaging in multilateral trade negotiations rather than unilateral actions

Harris has been critical of Trump's approach to trade, arguing that his tariff-based strategy hurt American consumers and farmers without achieving significant concessions from trading partners. She emphasizes the need for a more strategic approach that leverages America's alliances and economic strengths.

Donald Trump made trade a centerpiece of his economic policy, arguing that previous trade deals had disadvantaged American workers. His approach included:

- Renegotiating NAFTA into the USMCA (United States-Mexico-Canada Agreement)
- Imposing tariffs on a wide range of imports, particularly from China
- Withdrawing from the Trans-Pacific Partnership (TPP)
- Engaging in bilateral rather than multilateral trade negotiations

Trump argued that these actions would bring manufacturing jobs back to the United States and force trading partners to engage in fairer practices. Critics, however, pointed out that the tariffs often hurt American consumers and businesses, and that the trade wars created economic uncertainty.

The contrast between Harris and Trump on trade policy is notable. While Trump took a more confrontational, unilateral approach, Harris advocates for a return to multilateral engagement with a focus on enforcing labor and environmental standards. Her approach aims to harness the benefits of global trade while providing stronger protections for American workers and interests.

4. Small Business and Entrepreneurship

Small businesses are often described as the backbone of the American economy, and policies to support entrepreneurship can play a crucial role in driving innovation and job creation. Kamala Harris has proposed several measures to support small businesses and entrepreneurs.

Key elements of Harris's small business policy include:

- Expanding access to capital for small businesses, particularly those owned by women and minorities
- Strengthening the Small Business Administration's loan programs
- Providing tax credits for small businesses that create new jobs or increase wages
- Investing in technical assistance and mentorship programs for entrepreneurs
- Addressing the racial wealth gap by supporting Black-owned businesses

Harris emphasizes the need to level the playing field for small businesses, arguing that they often face barriers in accessing capital and competing with larger corporations.

Donald Trump's policies for small businesses focused primarily on tax cuts and deregulation. He argued that lowering the corporate tax rate and reducing regulatory burdens would benefit small businesses and encourage entrepreneurship. The Trump administration also expanded some Small Business Administration programs and provided support for small businesses during the COVID-19 pandemic through the Paycheck Protection Program.

While both Harris and Trump emphasize the importance of small businesses, their approaches differ. Harris's policies focus more on targeted support and addressing disparities, while Trump's approach relied more heavily on broad-based tax cuts and deregulation.

5. Infrastructure and Innovation

Investing in infrastructure and fostering innovation are crucial for long-term economic growth and competitiveness. Kamala Harris has proposed significant investments in both traditional and modern infrastructure.

Key elements of Harris's infrastructure and innovation plan include:

- Investing $10 trillion in infrastructure and clean energy over 10 years
- Upgrading transportation infrastructure, including roads, bridges, and public transit
- Expanding broadband access to rural and underserved areas
- Investing in research and development, particularly in areas like clean energy and biotechnology
- Promoting STEM education and workforce development in high-tech fields

Harris argues that these investments would not only create jobs in the short term but also enhance America's long-term economic competitiveness.

> *If you want to deal with an epidemic - crime or health - the smartest and most effective and cheapest way to deal with it is prevention first.*
>
> **Kamala Harris**

Donald Trump also emphasized the importance of infrastructure investment, proposing a $1 trillion infrastructure plan early in his presidency. However, this plan did not materialize into significant legislation. Trump's approach to innovation focused more on reducing regulations that he argued were stifling business creativity.

The contrast between Harris and Trump on infrastructure and innovation is primarily one of scale and focus. While both recognize the importance of infrastructure investment, Harris proposes a much larger investment with a particular emphasis on clean energy and addressing climate change. Her approach also places more emphasis on government's role in driving innovation through research and development funding.

6. Housing Policy

Access to affordable housing is a growing challenge in many parts of the country, with implications for economic mobility and quality of life. Kamala Harris has proposed several measures to address housing affordability and access.

Key elements of Harris's housing policy include:

- Providing a tax credit for renters paying more than 30% of their income on rent and utilities
- Investing $100 billion in assistance for homebuyers in historically redlined communities
- Expanding the Low-Income Housing Tax Credit to increase the supply of affordable housing
- Strengthening anti-discrimination laws in housing
- Addressing homelessness through supportive housing and services

Harris emphasizes the role of housing in economic security and the need to address historical disparities in homeownership.

Donald Trump's housing policy focused more on deregulation, arguing that reducing regulations would lower the cost of housing construction. His administration also sought to roll back some Obama-era fair housing rules, arguing they were overly burdensome.

The contrast between Harris and Trump on housing policy is significant. While Trump emphasized deregulation as the primary tool to address housing affordability, Harris proposes more direct government intervention through tax credits, investments, and strengthened regulations to promote fairness and affordability.

7. Economic Equity and Closing the Wealth Gap

Addressing economic inequality and closing the racial wealth gap are key priorities in Kamala Harris's economic agenda. She argues that these issues are not just matters of fairness, but are crucial for overall economic health and growth.

Key elements of Harris's economic equity policies include:

- Investing in historically black colleges and universities (HBCUs) and other minority-serving institutions
- Providing support for minority-owned businesses
- Addressing pay disparities, including strengthening equal pay laws
- Implementing baby bonds, a program that would provide every child with a savings account at birth
- Strengthening retirement security, including expanding Social Security

Harris emphasizes that addressing these disparities is crucial for unleashing the full economic potential of all Americans.

Donald Trump's approach to economic equity focused more on the idea that a rising tide lifts all boats. He pointed to low unemployment rates for minority groups prior to the pandemic as evidence that his economic policies were benefiting all Americans. However, critics argued that his policies did little to address underlying wealth and income disparities.

The contrast between Harris and Trump on economic equity is stark. While Trump relied primarily on overall economic growth to address disparities, Harris proposes targeted interventions to address historical and systemic inequalities.

8. Consumer Protection and Financial Regulation

The 2008 financial crisis highlighted the importance of robust consumer protection and financial regulation. Kamala Harris has been a strong advocate for consumer protection throughout her career.

Key elements of Harris's consumer protection and financial regulation policies include:

- Strengthening the Consumer Financial Protection Bureau (CFPB)
- Implementing stricter regulations on payday lenders
- Addressing student loan debt, including allowing refinancing of student loans
- Strengthening antitrust enforcement to promote competition
- Imposing stricter penalties for financial crimes

Harris argues that strong consumer protections and financial regulations are necessary to prevent predatory practices and ensure a stable economic system.

Donald Trump's administration took a different approach, generally favoring deregulation in the financial sector. This included rolling back some Dodd-Frank regulations and reducing the power of the CFPB. Trump argued that these regulations were overly burdensome and were stifling economic growth and lending.

The contrast between Harris and Trump on consumer protection and financial regulation is significant. While Trump emphasized deregulation to promote economic growth, Harris advocates for stronger protections and regulations to prevent abuses and ensure economic stability.

Conclusion

As we examine the economic policies of Kamala Harris and Donald Trump, we see two fundamentally different approaches to addressing America's economic challenges. Harris's policies generally reflect a more active role for government in shaping economic outcomes, addressing inequalities, and investing in long-term economic competitiveness. Her approach emphasizes equity, sustainability, and broad-based economic growth.

Key themes in Harris's economic agenda include:

1. A more progressive tax system that asks more from corporations and the wealthy
2. Significant investments in job creation, particularly in emerging sectors like clean energy
3. A focus on workers' rights and addressing wage stagnation
4. Targeted support for small businesses and entrepreneurs, particularly those from underrepresented groups
5. Large-scale investments in infrastructure and innovation
6. Addressing housing affordability through direct interventions
7. Targeted policies to address economic disparities and close the racial wealth gap
8. Strong consumer protections and financial regulations

Trump's economic policies, on the other hand, centered around tax cuts, deregulation, and a more confrontational approach to trade. His supporters argue that this approach led to strong economic growth and job creation prior to the pandemic, while critics contend that it exacerbated inequalities and prioritized short-term growth over long-term economic sustainability.

The choice between these economic visions is not just about policy details, but about fundamental questions of how the economy should work and who it should work for. Harris's policies reflect a view that government has a crucial role to play in shaping economic outcomes, addressing market failures, and ensuring that economic growth benefits all Americans. Trump's policies reflect a more traditional conservative view that emphasizes reducing government intervention and trusting market forces to drive economic growth.

As voters consider their choice for president, these contrasting economic visions provide a clear choice for the future direction of the country. Harris's economic agenda offers a path towards a more equitable and sustainable economy, with a focus on addressing long-standing disparities and investing in America's future competitiveness. While the feasibility of implementing all of these policies would depend on factors like Congressional support, they provide a clear roadmap for the direction in which Harris would seek to lead the country's economy.

In an era of growing inequality, technological disruption, and global economic challenges, Harris's economic policies offer a comprehensive approach to building a more prosperous and equitable America. Her vision seeks to harness the dynamism of the American economy while ensuring that its benefits are more broadly shared, positioning the United States for economic leadership in the 21st century.

Chapter 5

Foreign Policy and National Security
Restoring American Leadership

In an increasingly interconnected and complex world, a president's approach to foreign policy and national security can have profound implications not only for America's standing on the global stage but also for the safety and well-being of its citizens. This chapter will examine Kamala Harris's vision for America's role in the world, contrasting it with Donald Trump's "America First" approach, and explore why her policies may be better suited to address the global challenges of the 21st century.

1. Rebuilding Alliances and Multilateral Engagement

One of the cornerstones of Kamala Harris's foreign policy vision is the renewal and strengthening of America's traditional alliances and a return to robust multilateral engagement. Harris argues that many of the most pressing global challenges – from climate change and pandemics to terrorism and nuclear proliferation – require coordinated international action.

Key elements of Harris's approach to alliances and multilateralism include:

- Reaffirming America's commitment to NATO and other longstanding alliances
- Rejoining international agreements and organizations, such as the Paris Climate Accord and the World Health Organization
- Strengthening diplomatic ties with traditional allies in Europe and Asia
- Engaging more actively in multilateral forums like the United Nations
- Rebuilding the State Department and reinvesting in diplomacy

Harris contends that strong alliances and multilateral cooperation enhance America's security and influence, allowing the U.S. to tackle global challenges more effectively and share the burdens of international leadership.

In contrast, Donald Trump's "America First" foreign policy often put him at odds with traditional allies and international organizations. Trump was critical of NATO, arguing that other members weren't paying their fair share. He withdrew the U.S. from several international agreements, including the Paris Climate Accord and the Iran nuclear deal, and was often skeptical of multilateral approaches to global issues.

Trump argued that his approach put American interests first and that previous administrations had allowed other countries to take advantage of the U.S. in trade and security arrangements. However, critics contended that this approach weakened America's global influence and made it harder to address transnational challenges.

The contrast between Harris and Trump on this issue is stark. While Trump often viewed international relations through a transactional lens, Harris emphasizes the long-term strategic benefits of strong alliances and multilateral cooperation. Her approach aligns more closely with traditional U.S. foreign policy and the views of many foreign policy experts who argue that American leadership is most effective when exercised in concert with allies and through international institutions.

2. Addressing Global Challenges: Climate Change, Pandemics, and More

Kamala Harris views global challenges like climate change and pandemics as critical national security issues that require coordinated international action. Her approach emphasizes the interconnectedness of these issues and the need for American leadership in addressing them.

On climate change, Harris's policies include:

- Rejoining the Paris Climate Agreement and pushing for more ambitious global targets
- Investing in clean energy technology and sharing innovations with other countries
- Using diplomacy to encourage other nations to reduce their carbon emissions
- Addressing the security implications of climate change, including potential conflicts over resources and climate-driven migration

Regarding global health and pandemic preparedness, Harris advocates for:

- Strengthening the World Health Organization and other international health bodies
- Investing in global disease surveillance and early warning systems
- Coordinating international efforts to develop and distribute vaccines and treatments
- Addressing the economic and social impacts of pandemics on vulnerable populations

Harris also emphasizes the need to address other transnational challenges, such as cybersecurity threats, human trafficking, and global poverty.

Donald Trump's approach to these global challenges was markedly different. He withdrew the U.S. from the Paris Climate Agreement, arguing that it disadvantaged American workers and businesses. His administration rolled back many domestic environmental regulations and was skeptical of climate change science.

On global health, Trump was critical of the World Health Organization, particularly during the COVID-19 pandemic, and initiated the process of withdrawing the U.S. from the organization. His administration's pandemic response emphasized national measures over international cooperation.

The contrast between Harris and Trump on these issues reflects different views on the nature of global challenges and America's role in addressing them. While Trump often downplayed issues like climate change and emphasized national sovereignty in addressing global health threats, Harris sees these challenges as requiring coordinated international action with strong American leadership.

3. National Security and Defense Policy

While emphasizing diplomacy and multilateral cooperation, Kamala Harris also recognizes the importance of maintaining a strong national defense. Her approach to national security and defense policy seeks to balance military preparedness with diplomatic engagement and a broader conception of national security that includes economic and environmental factors.

Key elements of Harris's national security and defense policies include:

- Maintaining a strong, modern military while ending "forever wars"
- Emphasizing cyber security and addressing emerging threats in the digital realm
- Focusing on counterterrorism efforts that don't require large-scale troop deployments
- Reducing nuclear proliferation and extending arms control agreements
- Addressing the national security implications of climate change

Harris argues for a more holistic approach to national security that goes beyond traditional military concerns to include issues like economic security, cybersecurity, and climate resilience.

Donald Trump's approach to national security and defense was characterized by increases in military spending, skepticism of traditional arms control agreements, and a desire to reduce U.S. troop commitments overseas. He initiated negotiations with North Korea over its nuclear program, although these did not result in denuclearization.

Trump also ordered high-profile military actions, such as the strike that killed Iranian General Qasem Soleimani.

While both Harris and Trump emphasize the importance of a strong military, their approaches differ significantly. Trump's policies often prioritized unilateral action and military solutions, while Harris advocates for a more balanced approach that combines military strength with robust diplomacy and multilateral cooperation.

4. Trade and Economic Diplomacy

Kamala Harris views trade policy as a crucial component of both foreign policy and economic strategy. Her approach aims to balance the benefits of global trade with protections for American workers and strong labor and environmental standards.

Key aspects of Harris's trade policy include:

- Enforcing labor and environmental standards in trade agreements
- Addressing currency manipulation and other unfair trade practices
- Strengthening America's economic competitiveness through investments in education, research, and infrastructure
- Using trade policy as a tool to advance broader foreign policy goals, such as human rights and environmental protection

Harris criticizes what she sees as the overly confrontational and unilateral approach to trade taken by the Trump administration, arguing instead for a more strategic approach that leverages America's economic strengths and alliances.

Donald Trump made trade a centerpiece of his foreign policy, arguing that previous administrations had negotiated deals that disadvantaged American workers. His approach included:

- Imposing tariffs on a wide range of imports, particularly from China
- Renegotiating NAFTA into the USMCA (United States-Mexico-Canada Agreement)
- Withdrawing from the Trans-Pacific Partnership (TPP)
- Engaging in bilateral rather than multilateral trade negotiations

Trump argued that these actions would bring manufacturing jobs back to the United States and force trading partners to engage in fairer practices. Critics, however, pointed out that the tariffs often hurt American consumers and businesses, and that the trade wars created economic uncertainty.

The contrast between Harris and Trump on trade policy is significant. While Trump took a more confrontational, unilateral approach, Harris advocates for a return to multilateral engagement with a focus on enforcing labor and environmental standards. Her approach aims to harness the benefits of global trade while providing stronger protections for American workers and interests.

5. Human Rights and Democracy Promotion

Promoting human rights and democracy abroad has long been a stated goal of U.S. foreign policy, although administrations have varied in how much emphasis they place on these issues. Kamala Harris sees the promotion of human rights and democratic values as a core component of American foreign policy.

Key elements of Harris's approach to human rights and democracy promotion include:

- Using diplomatic and economic tools to pressure authoritarian regimes to improve their human rights records
- Supporting pro-democracy movements and civil society organizations in other countries
- Addressing human rights concerns in trade negotiations and other diplomatic engagements
- Strengthening international institutions that protect human rights and promote democracy

Harris argues that promoting human rights and democratic values not only aligns with America's moral principles but also serves its long-term strategic interests by fostering stability and creating allies that share U.S. values.

Donald Trump's approach to human rights and democracy promotion was more inconsistent. While his administration did impose sanctions on some countries for human rights abuses, Trump was also criticized for praising authoritarian leaders and downplaying human rights concerns in pursuit of other policy objectives. He often emphasized national sovereignty and non-intervention in the internal affairs of other countries.

The contrast between Harris and Trump on this issue is notable. While Trump often prioritized short-term strategic or economic interests over human rights concerns, Harris advocates for a foreign policy that more consistently emphasizes democratic values and human rights.

6. Middle East Policy

The Middle East remains a critical region for U.S. foreign policy, with ongoing conflicts, terrorism concerns, and energy interests shaping America's engagement in the area. Kamala Harris's approach to the Middle East seeks to balance security interests with diplomatic engagement and a commitment to human rights.

Key aspects of Harris's Middle East policy include:

- Supporting a two-state solution to the Israeli-Palestinian conflict
- Re-engaging with Iran diplomatically while maintaining pressure on its nuclear program
- Ending U.S. support for Saudi Arabia's military intervention in Yemen
- Maintaining counterterrorism efforts against groups like ISIS while avoiding large-scale troop deployments
- Promoting human rights and democratic reforms in the region

Harris criticizes what she sees as the Trump administration's overly militarized approach to the region and its unconditional support for certain allies despite human rights concerns.

Donald Trump's Middle East policy was marked by several significant moves, including:

- Moving the U.S. Embassy in Israel to Jerusalem and recognizing Israeli sovereignty over the Golan Heights
- Withdrawing from the Iran nuclear deal and imposing maximum pressure sanctions on Iran

- Brokering normalization agreements between Israel and several Arab states (the Abraham Accords)
- Ordering the strike that killed Iranian General Qasem Soleimani
- Maintaining close ties with Saudi Arabia despite concerns over human rights issues

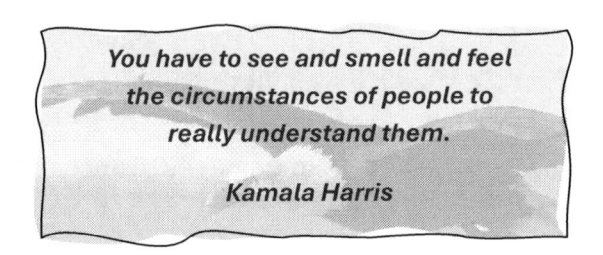

> *You have to see and smell and feel the circumstances of people to really understand them.*
>
> **Kamala Harris**

Trump argued that his approach brought new stability to the region and put pressure on adversaries like Iran. Critics, however, contended that his policies increased tensions in some areas and neglected long-standing issues like the Israeli-Palestinian conflict.

The contrast between Harris and Trump on Middle East policy is significant. While Trump's approach was characterized by bold unilateral actions and strong support for traditional U.S. allies in the region, Harris advocates for a more balanced approach that combines security cooperation with diplomatic engagement and a stronger emphasis on human rights.

7. China and the Asia-Pacific

The rise of China presents one of the most significant foreign policy challenges for the United States in the 21st century. Kamala Harris's approach to China and the broader Asia-Pacific region emphasizes strategic competition combined with cooperation on global challenges where interests align.

Key elements of Harris's China policy include:

- Strengthening alliances in the Asia-Pacific to counterbalance China's influence
- Addressing unfair trade practices and intellectual property theft through multilateral action
- Cooperating with China on global issues like climate change and pandemic response
- Criticizing China's human rights abuses, including its treatment of Uighurs and its actions in Hong Kong
- Maintaining a strong military presence in the region while avoiding unnecessary provocations

Harris argues for a nuanced approach that recognizes both the competitive and cooperative aspects of the U.S.-China relationship.

Donald Trump took a more confrontational approach to China, viewing it primarily as a strategic rival. Key aspects of Trump's China policy included:

- Imposing tariffs on Chinese goods as part of a broader trade war
- Restricting Chinese technology companies' access to U.S. markets
- Increasing freedom of navigation operations in the South China Sea
- Criticizing China's handling of the COVID-19 pandemic
- Taking a hard line on issues like Hong Kong and Taiwan

Trump argued that previous administrations had been too soft on China and that his tougher approach was necessary to protect American interests. Critics, however, contended that the confrontational strategy increased tensions without achieving significant concessions from China.

The contrast between Harris and Trump on China policy is notable. While both recognize the challenges posed by China's rise, Harris advocates for a more multilateral approach that balances competition with cooperation on global issues. Trump's approach was more unilateral and confrontational, viewing the relationship primarily through a competitive lens.

8. Russia and Eastern Europe

Relations with Russia and policy towards Eastern Europe represent another crucial area of U.S. foreign policy. Kamala Harris's approach to Russia emphasizes deterrence of aggression, support for NATO allies, and pushing back against Russian interference in democratic processes.

Key elements of Harris's Russia policy include:

- Maintaining and potentially increasing sanctions on Russia for its actions in Ukraine and election interference
- Strengthening NATO's eastern flank to deter Russian aggression
- Countering Russian disinformation and cyber operations
- Supporting democratic movements and civil society in Russia and former Soviet states
- Engaging in arms control negotiations while maintaining a strong deterrent

Harris argues for a firm stance towards Russia that combines diplomatic pressure, economic sanctions, and support for allies and democratic values.

Donald Trump's approach to Russia was a source of significant controversy throughout his presidency. While his administration did take some actions to counter Russian aggression, including imposing sanctions and providing military aid to Ukraine, Trump himself was often criticized for his conciliatory rhetoric towards Russian President Vladimir Putin. Key aspects of Trump's Russia policy included:

- Expressing skepticism about Russian interference in the 2016 election
- Calling for Russia to be readmitted to the G7
- Criticizing NATO allies for not meeting defense spending targets
- Withdrawing from the Intermediate-Range Nuclear Forces (INF) Treaty
- Engaging in direct diplomacy with Putin, including a controversial summit in Helsinki

Trump argued that better relations with Russia were in America's interest and that previous administrations' confrontational approaches had been counterproductive. Critics, however, contended that his approach emboldened Russian aggression and undermined the confidence of U.S. allies.

The contrast between Harris and Trump on Russia policy is stark. While Trump often seemed to seek improved relations with Russia despite its aggressive actions, Harris advocates for a more traditional approach of deterrence and support for allies, combined with targeted engagement on issues of mutual interest.

Conclusion

As we examine the foreign policy and national security positions of Kamala Harris and Donald Trump, we see two fundamentally different visions for America's role in the world. Harris's approach emphasizes rebuilding alliances, engaging in multilateral cooperation, and addressing global challenges through coordinated international action. Her policies reflect a belief in the importance of American leadership on the world stage, tempered by a recognition of the need for cooperation and coalition-building.

Key themes in Harris's foreign policy agenda include:

1. Rebuilding and strengthening traditional alliances
2. Addressing global challenges like climate change and pandemics through multilateral action
3. Balancing military strength with robust diplomacy
4. Pursuing trade policies that protect American workers while engaging in the global economy
5. Emphasizing human rights and democracy promotion
6. Taking a nuanced approach to complex relationships, such as those with China and Russia
7. Reaffirming America's commitment to international institutions and agreements

Trump's "America First" foreign policy, on the other hand, was characterized by skepticism of multilateral agreements and institutions, a more transactional approach to alliances, and a willingness to use unilateral action to pursue American interests. His supporters argue that this approach put American interests front and center and challenged the status quo in ways that benefited the U.S. Critics, however, contend that it weakened America's global standing, strained relationships with key allies, and made it harder to address transnational challenges.

The choice between these foreign policy visions is not just about specific policy positions, but about fundamental questions of how America should engage with the world and what role it should play in the international system. Harris's policies reflect a view that American interests are best served by robust international engagement, strong alliances, and leadership on global challenges. Trump's policies reflect a more nationalist view that emphasizes sovereignty and bilateral deal-making over multilateral cooperation.

As voters consider their choice for president, these contrasting foreign policy visions provide a clear choice for America's future role in the world. Harris's foreign policy agenda offers a path towards renewed American global leadership, with a focus on rebuilding alliances, addressing transnational challenges, and promoting democratic values. While the implementation of these policies would depend on various factors, including global events and domestic political considerations, they provide a clear roadmap for the direction in which Harris would seek to lead America's engagement with the world.

In an era of complex global challenges, shifting power dynamics, and rapid technological change, Harris's foreign policy approach offers a comprehensive strategy for maintaining America's global influence while addressing the interconnected threats of the 21st century. Her vision seeks to restore America's standing in the world, repair strained alliances, and position the United States to lead on critical global issues, from climate change to nuclear proliferation.

Chapter 6

Social Issues and Civil Rights
Towards a More Just and Equitable America

In an era marked by ongoing struggles for equality and social justice, a president's stance on social issues and civil rights can profoundly shape the nation's trajectory. This chapter will explore Kamala Harris's positions on key social issues and civil rights, contrasting them with Donald Trump's approach, and examine why her policies may be better suited to address the social challenges facing America today.

1. Racial Justice and Police Reform

The issue of racial justice, particularly in the context of law enforcement and the criminal justice system, has become a central concern in American politics. Kamala Harris, with her background as a prosecutor and her personal experience as a woman of color, brings a unique perspective to this issue.

Key elements of Harris's approach to racial justice and police reform include:

- Ending mandatory minimum sentences for non-violent drug offenses

- Banning chokeholds and no-knock warrants in federal law enforcement operations
- Creating a national registry of police officers who commit misconduct
- Investing in community-based alternatives to policing
- Addressing racial disparities in healthcare, education, and economic opportunity

Harris argues that systemic racism is a reality in America and that comprehensive reform is necessary to address it. She emphasizes the need for accountability in law enforcement while also recognizing the importance of public safety.

Donald Trump's approach to racial justice issues was markedly different. He often denied the existence of systemic racism and took a "law and order" stance on policing issues. Key aspects of Trump's approach included:

- Supporting law enforcement unconditionally and criticizing the Black Lives Matter movement
- Implementing the First Step Act, a bipartisan criminal justice reform bill
- Using federal law enforcement to quell protests in cities
- Ending federal racial sensitivity training, calling it "divisive"

Trump argued that his policies, such as opportunity zones and funding for historically black colleges and universities (HBCUs), did more for African Americans than previous administrations. Critics, however, contended that his rhetoric and policies exacerbated racial tensions and failed to address systemic issues.

The contrast between Harris and Trump on racial justice is stark. While Trump often downplayed racial issues and emphasized a "colorblind" approach, Harris acknowledges systemic racism and advocates for specific policies to address racial disparities. Her approach recognizes the complexity of these issues and the need for both reform and reconciliation.

2. LGBTQ+ Rights

The fight for LGBTQ+ equality has seen significant progress in recent years, but challenges remain. Kamala Harris has been a longtime advocate for LGBTQ+ rights and sees this as a crucial civil rights issue.

Key elements of Harris's LGBTQ+ rights agenda include:

- Passing the Equality Act to provide comprehensive anti-discrimination protections
- Supporting transgender rights, including in healthcare and military service
- Addressing violence against transgender individuals, particularly trans women of color
- Expanding access to PrEP and other HIV prevention and treatment methods
- Supporting LGBTQ+ youth, including efforts to combat homelessness and bullying

Harris argues that LGBTQ+ rights are human rights and that full equality under the law is essential for a just society.

Donald Trump's record on LGBTQ+ issues was mixed. While he claimed to be a friend to the LGBTQ+ community, many of his administration's policies were seen as rolling back LGBTQ+ protections. Key aspects of Trump's approach included:

- Banning transgender individuals from military service
- Allowing healthcare providers and adoption agencies to deny services based on religious beliefs
- Appointing conservative judges perceived as hostile to LGBTQ+ rights
- Removing protections for transgender students in schools

Trump argued that his policies protected religious freedom and maintained traditional values. Critics, however, saw these actions as undermining LGBTQ+ rights and enabling discrimination.

The contrast between Harris and Trump on LGBTQ+ rights is significant. While Trump's policies often aligned with conservative views on these issues, Harris advocates for expansive protections and full equality for LGBTQ+ individuals. Her approach aligns with the growing public support for LGBTQ+ rights and the view that this is a fundamental civil rights issue.

3. Women's Rights and Gender Equality

As potentially the first woman to serve as President of the United States, Kamala Harris brings a strong commitment to women's rights and gender equality to her policy agenda.

Key elements of Harris's approach to women's rights include:

- Protecting and expanding reproductive rights, including access to abortion

- Addressing the gender pay gap through increased transparency and enforcement
- Combating sexual harassment and assault, including strengthening Title IX protections
- Expanding paid family leave and access to affordable childcare
- Increasing women's representation in government and corporate leadership

Harris sees gender equality as essential for a just society and argues that women's rights are human rights.

Donald Trump's approach to women's issues was often controversial. While his administration implemented some policies aimed at supporting women, such as the Women's Global Development and Prosperity Initiative, he was frequently criticized for his rhetoric about women and some of his policy positions. Key aspects of Trump's approach included:

- Appointing conservative judges seen as hostile to abortion rights
- Reinstating and expanding the "global gag rule" on abortion counseling
- Rolling back Obama-era guidelines on campus sexual assault
- Implementing a paid family leave policy for federal workers

Trump argued that his economic policies benefited women by creating jobs and opportunities. Critics, however, pointed to his administration's efforts to restrict reproductive rights and his personal conduct as undermining women's equality.

The contrast between Harris and Trump on women's rights and gender equality is clear. While Trump's policies often aligned with conservative positions on these issues, Harris advocates for expansive protections for women's rights and sees gender equality as a core component of her policy agenda.

4. Immigration and Immigrant Rights

Immigration remains one of the most contentious issues in American politics. Kamala Harris, as the daughter of immigrants, brings a personal understanding to this issue and advocates for a compassionate yet secure approach to immigration policy.

Key elements of Harris's immigration policy include:

- Providing a path to citizenship for undocumented immigrants, including DACA recipients
- Reforming Immigration and Customs Enforcement (ICE), focusing on serious criminals rather than families
- Addressing the root causes of migration through aid and development in Central America
- Expanding legal immigration pathways, including for skilled workers and refugees
- Ending the practice of family separation at the border

Harris argues that America's diversity is its strength and that a fair and humane immigration system is essential for both moral and economic reasons.

Donald Trump made immigration a centerpiece of his political identity, campaigning on promises to build a wall on the U.S.-Mexico border and taking a hard line on both legal and illegal immigration. Key aspects of Trump's immigration policy included:

- Attempting to build a wall along the southern border
- Implementing a "zero tolerance" policy that led to family separations
- Imposing travel bans on several predominantly Muslim countries
- Reducing refugee admissions to historic lows
- Attempting to end the DACA program

Trump argued that these measures were necessary for national security and to protect American jobs. Critics contended that his policies were inhumane and contrary to American values.

The contrast between Harris and Trump on immigration is one of the starkest in their policy agendas. While Trump emphasized restriction and enforcement, often using harsh rhetoric about immigrants, Harris advocates for a more welcoming approach that balances security concerns with America's tradition as a nation of immigrants.

5. Gun Control

Gun violence remains a pressing issue in the United States, with mass shootings and everyday gun deaths continuing to shock the nation. Kamala Harris has been a strong advocate for what she calls "reasonable" gun control measures throughout her career.

Key elements of Harris's gun control policy include:

- Implementing universal background checks

- Banning assault weapons and high-capacity magazines
- Closing the "boyfriend loophole" to prevent domestic abusers from purchasing firearms
- Repealing the Protection of Lawful Commerce in Arms Act, which shields gun manufacturers from certain lawsuits
- Implementing a federal gun licensing program

Harris argues that these measures are necessary to address the epidemic of gun violence in America while respecting the Second Amendment rights of law-abiding citizens.

Donald Trump, backed by the National Rifle Association, took a strong pro-gun rights stance during his presidency. While he did ban bump stocks following the Las Vegas mass shooting, he generally opposed new gun control measures. Key aspects of Trump's approach to gun issues included:

- Opposing most new gun control measures, arguing they infringe on Second Amendment rights
- Emphasizing mental health and school security as solutions to mass shootings
- Appointing conservative judges likely to rule in favor of gun rights
- Declaring gun stores "essential businesses" during COVID-19 lockdowns

Trump argued that the focus should be on enforcing existing laws and addressing mental health issues rather than imposing new restrictions on gun ownership.

The contrast between Harris and Trump on gun control is significant. While Trump emphasized protecting gun ownership rights,

Harris advocates for what she sees as common-sense measures to reduce gun violence. Her position aligns more closely with public opinion polls that show majority support for measures like universal background checks.

6. Religious Freedom and Separation of Church and State

The balance between religious freedom and the separation of church and state remains a contentious issue in American politics. Kamala Harris advocates for a approach that protects religious freedom while maintaining a clear separation between religion and government.

Key elements of Harris's approach to religious issues include:

- Supporting the right to religious freedom while opposing discriminatory practices justified by religious beliefs
- Maintaining the Johnson Amendment, which prohibits tax-exempt organizations from endorsing political candidates
- Opposing the use of public funds for religious schools through voucher programs
- Supporting comprehensive sex education in schools rather than abstinence-only programs

Harris argues that religious freedom is a fundamental right, but that it should not be used as a justification for discrimination or to impose religious beliefs through government policy.

Donald Trump courted religious conservatives and took several actions aimed at appealing to this base. Key aspects of Trump's approach to religious issues included:

- Appointing conservative judges seen as sympathetic to religious freedom claims
- Implementing policies allowing healthcare providers to refuse services based on religious beliefs
- Expanding religious exemptions to contraception coverage mandates
- Attempting to repeal the Johnson Amendment

> *I was standing on a ladder outside the Homestead juvenile immigrant detention center outside Miami, looking over the fence, and I saw children lined up like prisoners. They had been separated from their families and put in this private detention facility. It was horrible.*
>
> *Kamala Harris*

Trump argued that his policies protected religious freedom and restored the role of faith in public life. Critics, however, saw many of these actions as undermining the separation of church and state and enabling discrimination under the guise of religious freedom.

The contrast between Harris and Trump on religious issues reflects different interpretations of the First Amendment and the role of religion in public life. While Trump often sought to blur the lines between church and state in ways that appealed to religious conservatives, Harris advocates for a clearer separation while still protecting individuals' right to religious belief and practice.

7. Voting Rights and Election Integrity

The issue of voting rights and election integrity has become increasingly contentious in recent years. Kamala Harris has been a strong advocate for expanding voting access and protecting the right to vote.

Key elements of Harris's approach to voting rights include:

- Supporting automatic voter registration and same-day registration
- Restoring voting rights to felons who have completed their sentences
- Opposing voter ID laws that she sees as discriminatory
- Expanding early voting and vote-by-mail options
- Strengthening the Voting Rights Act

Harris argues that the right to vote is fundamental to democracy and that efforts should be made to make voting as accessible as possible while maintaining election integrity.

Donald Trump, particularly following his loss in the 2020 election, focused heavily on claims of voter fraud and election security. Key aspects of Trump's approach to voting issues included:

- Making unsubstantiated claims of widespread voter fraud
- Supporting stricter voter ID laws
- Opposing expanded mail-in voting
- Criticizing the security of voting machines and election processes

Trump argued that strict measures were necessary to ensure election integrity. Critics, however, contended that many of these measures were unnecessary and aimed at suppressing voter turnout, particularly among minority communities.

The contrast between Harris and Trump on voting rights is significant. While Trump emphasized potential fraud and supported measures that critics saw as restrictive, Harris advocates for expanding access to voting and sees many of the restrictive measures as forms of voter suppression.

8. Education and Student Debt

Education policy, including the issue of student debt, has become a major concern for many Americans. Kamala Harris sees education as a key tool for addressing inequality and preparing Americans for the jobs of the future.

Key elements of Harris's education policy include:

- Making community college free for all Americans
- Increasing teacher pay by an average of $13,500
- Expanding access to early childhood education
- Supporting debt-free college for students from families earning less than $125,000 per year
- Cancelling up to $20,000 in student loan debt for Pell Grant recipients who start a business in disadvantaged communities

Harris argues that investing in education is crucial for economic growth and social mobility.

Donald Trump's education policies focused primarily on expanding school choice through measures like charter schools and voucher programs. Key aspects of Trump's approach to education included:

- Promoting school choice and voucher programs

- Reducing federal regulations on schools
- Emphasizing patriotic education and criticizing "critical race theory"
- Pausing federal student loan payments during the COVID-19 pandemic

Trump argued that his policies would improve educational outcomes by increasing competition and reducing bureaucracy. Critics, however, contended that many of these measures would undermine public education and exacerbate educational inequalities.

The contrast between Harris and Trump on education policy is notable. While Trump emphasized market-based solutions and local control, Harris advocates for a more active federal role in addressing educational inequities and ensuring access to quality education at all levels.

Conclusion

As we examine the positions of Kamala Harris and Donald Trump on social issues and civil rights, we see two fundamentally different visions for America's future. Harris's policies generally reflect a more expansive view of civil rights and social justice, emphasizing the need to address systemic inequalities and protect the rights of marginalized groups. Her approach is characterized by:

1. A recognition of systemic racism and the need for comprehensive police reform
2. Strong support for LGBTQ+ rights and gender equality
3. A compassionate yet secure approach to immigration
4. Advocacy for gun control measures to address gun violence

5. Support for a clear separation of church and state while protecting religious freedom
6. A focus on expanding voting rights and access
7. Emphasis on education as a tool for social mobility and economic growth

Trump's policies, on the other hand, often aligned more closely with conservative positions on these issues. His approach was characterized by:

1. Skepticism of systemic racism claims and a "law and order" approach to policing
2. More traditional views on LGBTQ+ issues and gender roles
3. A restrictive approach to immigration with an emphasis on enforcement
4. Strong support for gun ownership rights
5. Efforts to appeal to religious conservatives through policy actions
6. Focus on claims of voter fraud and support for more restrictive voting measures
7. Emphasis on school choice and local control in education

The choice between these visions is not just about policy details, but about fundamental questions of what kind of society America should be and how to balance competing rights and interests. Harris's policies reflect a view that government has a crucial role to play in protecting civil rights, addressing systemic inequalities, and ensuring equal opportunity for all Americans. Trump's policies reflect a more traditional conservative view that emphasizes individual responsibility, limited government intervention, and the preservation of traditional social norms.

As voters consider their choice for president, these contrasting visions on social issues and civil rights provide a clear choice for the future direction of the country. Harris's agenda offers a path towards a more inclusive and equitable society, with a focus on addressing long-standing disparities and expanding protections for civil rights. While the feasibility of implementing all of these policies would depend on factors like Congressional support, they provide a clear roadmap for the direction in which Harris would seek to lead the country on these critical issues.

In an era of ongoing struggles for equality and social justice, Harris's approach to social issues and civil rights offers a comprehensive strategy for addressing systemic inequalities and moving towards a more just and equitable America. Her vision seeks to expand the promise of American democracy to all citizens, regardless of race, gender, sexual orientation, or background, while navigating the complex challenges of balancing competing rights and interests in a diverse society.

Chapter 7

Environmental Policy and Climate Change
Securing a Sustainable Future

In an era where the impacts of climate change are becoming increasingly evident and urgent, a president's stance on environmental policy and climate action can have far-reaching consequences not just for the United States, but for the entire planet. This chapter will explore Kamala Harris's positions on environmental issues and climate change, contrasting them with Donald Trump's approach, and examine why her policies may be better suited to address the environmental challenges facing America and the world today.

1. Climate Change: A Comprehensive Approach

Kamala Harris views climate change as one of the most pressing issues of our time, requiring immediate and decisive action. She sees it not just as an environmental challenge, but as a threat to national security, public health, and economic stability.

Key elements of Harris's climate change policy include:

- Achieving net-zero emissions by 2050
- Investing $10 trillion in clean energy and infrastructure over 10 years

- Rejoining the Paris Climate Agreement and pushing for more ambitious global targets
- Implementing a carbon tax with proceeds invested in clean energy and climate resilience
- Creating millions of green jobs in renewable energy, sustainable agriculture, and conservation

Harris argues that addressing climate change is not only necessary to prevent catastrophic environmental damage but also presents an opportunity to revolutionize the American economy and create millions of well-paying jobs.

Donald Trump, in contrast, was skeptical of climate change science and pursued policies that prioritized fossil fuel production and rolled back environmental regulations. Key aspects of Trump's climate policy included:

- Withdrawing from the Paris Climate Agreement
- Rolling back Obama-era emissions standards for vehicles
- Promoting coal, oil, and natural gas production
- Reducing the size of national monuments to allow for more resource extraction
- Questioning the scientific consensus on climate change

Trump argued that environmental regulations were hurting American businesses and workers, particularly in industries like coal mining. He framed his policies as protecting American jobs and energy independence.

The contrast between Harris and Trump on climate change could not be starker. While Trump questioned the science of climate change and prioritized short-term economic considerations, Harris sees addressing climate change as both an environmental imperative and an economic opportunity. Her approach aligns more closely with the scientific consensus on the urgency of addressing climate change and the growing public concern about this issue.

2. Clean Energy and Green Technology

Central to Kamala Harris's climate strategy is a massive investment in clean energy and green technology. She sees this as a way to simultaneously address climate change, create jobs, and position the United States as a leader in the industries of the future.

Key aspects of Harris's clean energy policy include:

- Achieving 100% carbon-neutral electricity by 2035
- Investing in research and development of renewable energy technologies
- Providing incentives for the adoption of electric vehicles and charging infrastructure
- Supporting the development of energy storage technologies
- Investing in smart grid technology to improve energy efficiency

Harris argues that these investments will not only help combat climate change but will also create millions of well-paying jobs and ensure America's competitiveness in the global economy.

Donald Trump, on the other hand, was a strong advocate for traditional fossil fuel industries. His administration:

- Rolled back regulations on coal-fired power plants

- Opened up new areas for oil and gas drilling, including in the Arctic National Wildlife Refuge
- Reduced fuel efficiency standards for automobiles
- Criticized renewable energy sources, particularly wind power, as unreliable and expensive

Trump argued that his policies were protecting American energy jobs and ensuring energy independence. Critics, however, pointed out that his approach was out of step with global trends towards renewable energy and risked leaving the U.S. behind in the development of green technologies.

The contrast between Harris and Trump on clean energy is significant. While Trump sought to prop up declining fossil fuel industries, Harris proposes a forward-looking strategy that embraces the global shift towards renewable energy. Her approach aligns with economic forecasts that predict significant growth in clean energy sectors in the coming decades.

3. Environmental Protection and Conservation

Beyond climate change, Kamala Harris has a comprehensive environmental protection agenda that aims to conserve natural resources, protect biodiversity, and ensure clean air and water for all Americans.

Key elements of Harris's environmental protection policies include:

- Strengthening the Environmental Protection Agency (EPA) and reversing Trump-era deregulation
- Protecting and expanding national parks and monuments

- Addressing environmental justice issues in low-income communities and communities of color
- Protecting endangered species and biodiversity
- Implementing stricter regulations on pollutants and toxic chemicals

Harris argues that environmental protection is crucial for public health, quality of life, and the long-term sustainability of the American economy.

Donald Trump's approach to environmental protection was characterized by deregulation and a focus on resource extraction. Key aspects of his environmental policy included:

- Reducing the size of national monuments like Bears Ears and Grand Staircase-Escalante
- Rolling back Clean Water Act protections
- Weakening the Endangered Species Act
- Reducing EPA enforcement actions against polluters
- Opening up more federal lands for drilling and mining

Trump argued that these actions were necessary to reduce regulatory burdens on businesses and promote economic growth. Critics, however, contended that they put short-term economic interests ahead of long-term environmental sustainability and public health.

The contrast between Harris and Trump on environmental protection is clear. While Trump prioritized deregulation and resource extraction, Harris advocates for stronger environmental protections and conservation efforts. Her approach aligns more closely with the views of environmental scientists and advocates who argue that robust environmental protections are crucial for long-term sustainability and public health.

4. Water Policy and Infrastructure

Access to clean water is a fundamental human need and a critical environmental issue. Kamala Harris has proposed comprehensive policies to address water infrastructure, conservation, and access.

Key elements of Harris's water policy include:

- Investing in upgrading America's water infrastructure, including replacing lead pipes
- Addressing water scarcity issues, particularly in the Western United States
- Protecting water resources from pollution and contamination
- Ensuring access to clean, affordable water for all communities
- Implementing water conservation measures and promoting water-efficient technologies

Harris sees water policy as a critical environmental and public health issue, as well as an opportunity for infrastructure investment and job creation.

Donald Trump's water policy focused primarily on rolling back regulations and promoting water access for agriculture and industry. Key aspects of his approach included:

- Repealing the Obama-era Waters of the United States rule
- Promoting water access for farmers, particularly in California's Central Valley

- Criticizing water efficiency standards for appliances and fixtures
- Reducing federal oversight of water pollution

Trump argued that his policies would benefit farmers and reduce regulatory burdens. Critics, however, contended that his approach weakened crucial protections for water resources and failed to address long-term water sustainability issues.

The contrast between Harris and Trump on water policy reflects their broader differences on environmental issues. While Trump focused on reducing regulations and promoting short-term access, Harris advocates for a more comprehensive approach that balances current needs with long-term sustainability and public health concerns.

5. Sustainable Agriculture and Food Policy

Agriculture plays a crucial role in both the American economy and its environmental impact. Kamala Harris has proposed policies aimed at promoting sustainable agriculture practices while supporting farmers and rural communities.

Key elements of Harris's agricultural and food policy include:

- Investing in sustainable and regenerative farming practices
- Supporting small and medium-sized farms, particularly those owned by people of color
- Promoting soil health and carbon sequestration in agriculture
- Addressing food insecurity and promoting access to healthy foods

- Reducing food waste and promoting more sustainable food systems

Harris argues that these policies can help address climate change, support rural economies, and improve public health.

Donald Trump's agricultural policies focused more on traditional farming practices and supporting large agribusinesses. Key aspects of his approach included:

- Providing subsidies and aid to farmers affected by trade disputes
- Rolling back regulations on pesticide use and genetically modified organisms (GMOs)
- Promoting increased agricultural exports
- Reducing nutritional standards for school lunches

Trump argued that his policies were supporting American farmers and reducing regulatory burdens. Critics, however, contended that his approach favored large agribusinesses over small farmers and failed to address the environmental impacts of industrial agriculture.

The contrast between Harris and Trump on agricultural policy is significant. While Trump emphasized traditional farming practices and support for large agribusinesses, Harris advocates for a shift towards more sustainable practices and support for smaller, more diverse farming operations. Her approach aligns more closely with environmental concerns about the impact of industrial agriculture and the need for more sustainable food systems.

6. Environmental Justice

Environmental justice - the fair treatment and meaningful involvement of all people regardless of race, color, national origin, or income with respect to environmental laws and policies - is a key component of Kamala Harris's environmental agenda.

Key elements of Harris's environmental justice policies include:

- Addressing the disproportionate impact of pollution and climate change on low-income communities and communities of color
- Ensuring that these communities have a voice in environmental decision-making
- Investing in clean-up and remediation efforts in areas affected by industrial pollution
- Promoting green spaces and access to nature in urban areas
- Addressing the health impacts of environmental pollution in vulnerable communities

Harris argues that environmental justice is a critical civil rights issue and that addressing environmental inequities is crucial for building a fair and sustainable society.

Donald Trump's administration largely dismantled environmental justice initiatives. Key aspects of his approach included:

- Reducing funding for EPA environmental justice programs
- Rolling back regulations that disproportionately impacted vulnerable communities
- Promoting industrial development without significant consideration of environmental justice concerns

Trump argued that his pro-business policies would create jobs in all communities. Critics, however, pointed out that his policies often exacerbated environmental inequalities and ignored the concerns of vulnerable communities.

> DACA recipients risk a lot to come out of the shadows & sign up, but many will tell you the risk is worth being able to live and work in the only country they've ever known as home. DACA recipients serve in our military, work in Fortune 100 companies, and conduct important medical research.
>
> **Kamala Harris**

The contrast between Harris and Trump on environmental justice is stark. While Trump's policies often ignored or exacerbated environmental inequalities, Harris places environmental justice at the center of her environmental agenda. Her approach aligns with growing recognition of the intersectionality of environmental and social justice issues.

7. Ocean Conservation and Coastal Protection

With its vast coastlines and economic reliance on ocean resources, ocean conservation and coastal protection are critical issues for the United States. Kamala Harris has proposed comprehensive policies to address these challenges.

Key elements of Harris's ocean and coastal policies include:

- Protecting and expanding marine protected areas
- Addressing ocean acidification and marine pollution
- Promoting sustainable fisheries and aquaculture

- Investing in coastal resilience to address sea-level rise and extreme weather events
- Supporting research on ocean health and marine ecosystems

Harris sees ocean conservation as crucial for both environmental sustainability and the economic health of coastal communities.

Donald Trump's policies often prioritized coastal development and resource extraction over conservation. Key aspects of his approach included:

- Opening up previously protected coastal areas for offshore drilling
- Reducing the size of marine national monuments
- Weakening offshore drilling safety regulations
- Withdrawing from the Paris Agreement, which addresses ocean acidification

Trump argued that these policies would promote energy independence and economic development. Critics, however, contended that they posed significant risks to marine ecosystems and coastal communities.

The contrast between Harris and Trump on ocean and coastal policy is significant. While Trump often prioritized short-term economic considerations over long-term sustainability, Harris advocates for a more balanced approach that recognizes the long-term economic value of healthy marine ecosystems.

8. International Environmental Leadership

Kamala Harris recognizes that environmental challenges, particularly climate change, are global issues that require international cooperation. She advocates for the United States to reassert its role as a global leader in environmental protection and climate action.

Key elements of Harris's approach to international environmental issues include:

- Rejoining the Paris Climate Agreement and pushing for more ambitious global targets
- Engaging in international efforts to protect biodiversity and combat deforestation
- Promoting the export of American clean energy technologies
- Addressing the national security implications of climate change
- Supporting climate adaptation efforts in developing countries

Harris argues that U.S. leadership is crucial for effective global action on environmental issues and that this leadership also presents economic opportunities for American businesses.

Donald Trump took a more isolationist approach to international environmental issues. Key aspects of his policy included:

- Withdrawing from the Paris Climate Agreement
- Reducing U.S. contributions to international environmental efforts
- Criticizing other countries' environmental records while downplaying U.S. responsibilities

- Focusing on domestic energy production over global environmental concerns

Trump argued that international environmental agreements disadvantaged the U.S. economically. Critics, however, contended that his approach undermined global efforts to address critical environmental challenges and ceded leadership to other countries, particularly China.

The contrast between Harris and Trump on international environmental leadership is clear. While Trump retreated from international environmental commitments, Harris advocates for the U.S. to reclaim its role as a global leader on these issues. Her approach aligns with the views of many foreign policy experts who argue that environmental leadership is crucial for America's global influence and long-term strategic interests.

Conclusion

As we examine the environmental policies of Kamala Harris and Donald Trump, we see two fundamentally different visions for America's environmental future and its role in addressing global environmental challenges. Harris's policies reflect a comprehensive approach to environmental protection and climate action, recognizing these issues as critical for both the planet's health and America's long-term prosperity. Her approach is characterized by:

1. Ambitious targets for reducing greenhouse gas emissions and transitioning to clean energy
2. Large-scale investments in green technology and infrastructure

3. A commitment to environmental justice and addressing disparities in environmental impacts
4. Strong support for conservation efforts and biodiversity protection
5. Recognition of the economic opportunities presented by the transition to a green economy
6. A holistic approach that connects environmental issues to public health, national security, and economic policy
7. A commitment to reasserting U.S. leadership on global environmental issues

Trump's environmental policies, on the other hand, often prioritized short-term economic considerations and traditional industries over long-term environmental sustainability. His approach was characterized by:

1. Skepticism of climate change science and withdrawal from international climate agreements
2. Rolling back environmental regulations to reduce burdens on businesses
3. Promoting fossil fuel production and use
4. Reducing the size and scope of protected lands and waters
5. Downplaying environmental justice concerns
6. Focusing on traditional measures of economic growth over environmental considerations
7. A more isolationist approach to global environmental challenges

The choice between these environmental visions is not just about policy details, but about fundamental questions of how we value our natural resources, how we understand the relationship between environmental health and economic prosperity, and what responsibility we believe the United States has in addressing global environmental challenges.

Harris's policies reflect a view that robust environmental protection and aggressive action on climate change are not only necessary for the planet's health but are also crucial for America's long-term economic competitiveness and national security. Her approach aligns more closely with the scientific consensus on environmental issues and the growing public concern about climate change.

Trump's policies reflected a more traditional view that often saw environmental protection as being in conflict with economic growth. His approach appealed to those who were concerned about the economic impacts of environmental regulations, particularly in industries like coal mining and oil and gas extraction.

As voters consider their choice for president, these contrasting environmental visions provide a clear choice for America's future approach to these critical issues. Harris's environmental agenda offers a path towards a more sustainable future, with a focus on addressing the urgent threat of climate change while also creating new economic opportunities in clean energy and green technology. While the feasibility of implementing all of these policies would depend on factors like Congressional support, they provide a clear roadmap for the direction in which Harris would seek to lead the country on environmental issues.

In an era where the impacts of climate change are becoming increasingly evident and the need for environmental action more urgent, Harris's comprehensive approach to environmental policy offers a strategy for addressing these challenges while positioning the United States as a leader in the green technologies and industries of the future. Her vision seeks to balance environmental protection with economic opportunity, addressing current environmental challenges while laying the groundwork for a more sustainable and prosperous future.

Conclusion

The Choice for America's Future

As we conclude our comprehensive examination of Kamala Harris's candidacy in comparison to Donald Trump's presidency, it's clear that the choice between these two leaders represents far more than a simple political preference. It embodies two fundamentally different visions for America's future, touching on every aspect of governance, society, and the nation's role in the world.

Throughout this book, we've explored seven key areas where the contrasts between Harris and Trump are particularly stark: experience and qualifications, leadership style and character, domestic policy, economic policy, foreign policy and national security, social issues and civil rights, and environmental policy and climate change. Let's briefly recap these differences and consider their implications for the future of the United States.

1. Experience and Qualifications

Kamala Harris brings to the table a wealth of experience in public service, having served as a District Attorney, Attorney General of California, U.S. Senator, and Vice President. This diverse background has given her a comprehensive understanding of governance at local, state, and federal levels. Her legal expertise and experience in executive roles provide her with valuable skills for navigating the complexities of the presidency.

Donald Trump, in contrast, came to the presidency with a background in business and reality television, but no prior experience in government or public service. While his supporters argued that his outsider status was an asset, his presidency demonstrated the challenges that can arise from a lack of political experience.

The implications of this difference are significant. Harris's experience suggests she would be better prepared to navigate the intricacies of government, understand the nuances of policy-making, and manage the complex responsibilities of the presidency from day one.

2. Leadership Style and Character

Harris has demonstrated a collaborative leadership style throughout her career, showing an ability to work across party lines and build coalitions. She emphasizes empathy, emotional intelligence, and inclusivity in her approach to leadership. Her adaptability and willingness to evolve her positions based on new information suggest a leader who can navigate the complex and changing challenges of the modern world.

Trump's leadership style was often characterized as more confrontational and divisive. His approach was often described as intuitive and based on personal relationships rather than formal processes. While this unconventional style energized his base, it also led to frequent conflicts with other branches of government, the media, and even members of his own administration.

The choice between these leadership styles has profound implications for how the country would be governed. Harris's approach suggests a presidency focused on unity, collaboration, and measured decision-making, while Trump's style points to a more unpredictable and polarizing governance.

3. Domestic Policy

On domestic issues, Harris and Trump offer starkly different visions. Harris advocates for expanded healthcare access, comprehensive immigration reform, stricter gun control measures, and policies aimed at addressing systemic inequalities. She sees a strong role for government in addressing societal challenges and ensuring equal opportunity for all Americans.

Trump's domestic policies generally aligned with traditional conservative positions, emphasizing deregulation, tax cuts, and a more restrictive approach to immigration. He often framed issues like healthcare and gun rights in terms of individual choice and limited government intervention.

The implications of these differing approaches to domestic policy are far-reaching, potentially affecting everything from healthcare access and economic inequality to immigration and civil rights. The choice between Harris and Trump represents a fundamental decision about the role of government in addressing societal issues and shaping the nation's future.

4. Economic Policy

Harris's economic vision focuses on addressing income inequality, supporting the middle class, and creating opportunities for disadvantaged communities. She proposes significant investments in infrastructure, education, and clean energy, funded in part by increased taxes on corporations and high-income individuals. Her policies emphasize the need for a more equitable economy that works for all Americans.

Trump's economic approach centered around tax cuts and deregulation, arguing that these measures would stimulate economic growth and job creation. His policies often favored traditional industries and emphasized short-term economic indicators like stock market performance.

The choice between these economic visions has significant implications for the future of the American economy. Harris's approach suggests a focus on long-term, sustainable growth and addressing economic disparities, while Trump's policies prioritize immediate growth and traditional economic measures.

5. Foreign Policy and National Security

In the realm of foreign policy, Harris advocates for rebuilding international alliances, engaging in multilateral cooperation, and reasserting American leadership on global issues like climate change. She emphasizes diplomacy and sees America's diversity as a strength in international relations.

Trump's "America First" foreign policy was characterized by skepticism of multilateral agreements and institutions, a more transactional approach to alliances, and a willingness to use unilateral action to pursue American interests. He often questioned the value of traditional alliances and international organizations.

The implications of these differing approaches to foreign policy are profound, potentially reshaping America's role in the world and its relationships with both allies and adversaries. The choice between Harris and Trump represents a decision about whether the U.S. will seek to lead through multilateral cooperation or pursue a more unilateral and transactional approach to international relations.

6. Social Issues and Civil Rights

On social issues and civil rights, Harris and Trump again offer contrasting visions. Harris advocates for expansive civil rights protections, including strong support for LGBTQ+ rights, racial justice, and gender equality. She sees addressing systemic inequalities as a crucial government responsibility.

Trump's approach to social issues often aligned with more conservative positions. His administration rolled back several Obama-era civil rights protections and took a "law and order" approach to issues of racial justice.

The choice between these approaches has significant implications for the direction of social progress in America. It represents a fundamental decision about how the country will address issues of equality, justice, and civil rights in the coming years.

7. Environmental Policy and Climate Change

Perhaps nowhere is the contrast between Harris and Trump more stark than on environmental issues and climate change. Harris sees climate change as an existential threat requiring urgent action. She proposes ambitious targets for reducing emissions, massive investments in clean energy, and reasserting U.S. leadership in global climate efforts.

Trump, on the other hand, was skeptical of climate change science and pursued policies that prioritized fossil fuel production and rolled back environmental regulations. He withdrew the U.S. from the Paris Climate Agreement and often framed environmental protection as being in conflict with economic growth.

The implications of this difference cannot be overstated. The choice between Harris and Trump represents a critical decision about how the U.S. will address the urgent threat of climate change and shape its environmental future.

Synthesis and Implications

When we step back and look at these seven areas holistically, we see two fundamentally different visions for America's future. Harris represents a progressive vision that emphasizes government's role in addressing societal challenges, promoting equality, and leading on global issues. Her approach is characterized by a belief in the power of diversity, the importance of science and expertise, and the need for bold action to address long-standing issues and emerging threats.

Trump, on the other hand, represented a more traditional conservative vision that emphasized limited government, individual responsibility, and a more nationalist approach to international relations. His presidency was characterized by a willingness to challenge established norms and institutions, a skepticism of scientific consensus on issues like climate change, and a focus on short-term economic growth over long-term sustainability.

The choice between these visions has profound implications for the future of the United States and, indeed, the world. It will shape how the country addresses critical issues like climate change, economic inequality, and racial justice. It will influence America's role on the global stage and its relationships with both allies and adversaries. And it will set the tone for political discourse and social progress for years to come.

Moreover, this choice comes at a critical juncture in American history. The country faces numerous challenges, from the ongoing impacts of the COVID-19 pandemic to growing economic inequality, from the urgent threat of climate change to a reckoning with systemic racism. The leader chosen to navigate these challenges will play a crucial role in shaping America's future trajectory.

Harris's candidacy also represents a historic opportunity. As a woman of color, her election would break significant barriers and send a powerful message about representation and opportunity in America. This symbolic aspect of her candidacy should not be underestimated; it has the potential to inspire a new generation of leaders and reshape perceptions of what is possible in American politics.

It's important to note that the implementation of either leader's vision would depend on numerous factors, including Congressional support, global events, and economic conditions. No president can unilaterally reshape the country according to their vision. However, the president plays a crucial role in setting the national agenda, shaping public discourse, and making key decisions that can have long-lasting impacts.

As voters consider their choice, it's crucial to look beyond partisan labels and carefully consider the implications of each candidate's vision for the country's future. This decision is not just about the next four years, but about the long-term direction of the United States.

In making this choice, voters should consider not only their own interests but also the kind of country they want to leave for future generations. They should think about the values they believe should guide the nation and the role they believe America should play in the world.

It's also important to approach this decision with a critical and discerning eye. No candidate is perfect, and it's crucial to honestly assess the strengths and weaknesses of each. Voters should seek out reliable information, fact-check claims, and be willing to engage with viewpoints different from their own.

In conclusion, the choice between Kamala Harris and Donald Trump represents more than just a political preference. It is a choice about the future of American democracy, the direction of its society, and its role in the world. It is a decision that will shape the lives of Americans for years to come and have ripple effects across the globe.

As we've argued throughout this book, Kamala Harris offers a vision for America that is progressive, inclusive, and forward-looking. Her experience, leadership style, and policy positions suggest a presidency that would seek to unite rather than divide, to build rather than tear down, and to lead with empathy, integrity, and a commitment to democratic values.

However, the ultimate decision lies with the American people. It is their responsibility, and their right, to carefully consider the options before them and choose the leader they believe will best guide the nation through the challenges and opportunities that lie ahead.

As we conclude this exploration of Kamala Harris's candidacy, we hope that this book has provided valuable insights and a framework for understanding the critical choice facing the nation. Regardless of the outcome, this election will be a defining moment in American history. It is up to each citizen to engage in this process, to make their voice heard, and to help shape the future of their country.

The power of democracy lies in the hands of informed citizens. Your vote is your voice, and it matters. The future of the nation depends on it.

Appendices

Appendix A: Fact-Checking Resources

In the age of misinformation and "fake news," it's crucial for voters to verify the claims made by candidates and their campaigns. Here are some reliable fact-checking resources:

1. FactCheck.org - A nonpartisan, nonprofit "consumer advocate" for voters run by the Annenberg Public Policy Center of the University of Pennsylvania.
2. PolitiFact.com - A Pulitzer Prize-winning website run by the Poynter Institute that rates the accuracy of claims by elected officials and others on its Truth-O-Meter.
3. Washington Post Fact Checker - Assesses the accuracy of claims by politicians and awards "Pinocchios" based on the level of falsehood.
4. Snopes.com - One of the internet's oldest fact-checking websites, known for debunking urban legends and political claims.
5. Reuters Fact Check - A global team of Reuters journalists who verify social media posts and visual content.

Remember to cross-reference multiple sources and be aware of potential biases in all media outlets.

Appendix B: Timeline of Kamala Harris's Political Career

This timeline provides a chronological overview of Kamala Harris's journey in public service:

1990: Joins Alameda County District Attorney's Office
2003: Elected District Attorney of San Francisco
2010: Elected Attorney General of California
2016: Elected to the United States Senate
2019: Launches presidential campaign
2020: Selected as Joe Biden's running mate and elected Vice President

Senator Kamala Harris
Kavanaugh Confirmation Hearing Opening Statement
September 4, 2018

So I thank you, Mr. Chairman. I'd like to restate my objection from earlier for the record, which is my motion to postpone this hearing. A number of comments have been made by my honored and respected colleagues. I'd like to address a few of them.

One, there was some mention of a concern about Elena Kagan's hearing and that the White House at the time, there was an agreement that those certain records are sensitive and should therefore not be disclosed. It's my understanding that as a point of distinction between that time and today, that those were active cases in the White House and for that reason there was an understanding and agreement that they were of a sensitive nature and should not be disclosed.

In terms of the point that has been made about playing politics and blaming the Supreme Court, I think that we have to give pause when those kinds of concerns are expressed to also think about the fact that there have been many a political campaign that has been run indicating an intention to use the United States Supreme Court as a political tool to end things like the Affordable Care Act, the Voting Rights Act, and campaign finance reform. Which makes this conversation a legitimate one in terms of a reasoned concern about whether this nominee has been nominated to fulfill a political agenda, as it relates to using that Court and the use of that Court.

As it relates to the 42,000 documents, or 42,000 pages of documents, I find it interesting that we get those documents less than 24 hours before this hearing is scheduled to begin, but it took 57 days for those documents to be vetted before we would even be given those documents. So there is some suggestion that we should be speed-readers, and read 42,000 pages of documents in about 15 hours, when it took the other side 57 days to review those same documents. So the logic at least on the math is not applying.

Now, the Chairman has requested 10% of the nominee's documents. That's 10% of 100% of his full record.

The nominee's personal lawyer has only given us 7% of his documents. 7% out of 100% of the full record.

Republicans have only given 4% of these records or made them public. That's 4% of 100% of a full record.

96% of his record is missing. 96% of his record is missing. It is reasonable, it is reasonable that we should want to review his entire record and then we can debate among us the relevance of what is in his record to his nomination, but it should not be the ability of the leadership of this committee to unilaterally make decisions about what we will and will not see in terms of its admissibility, instead of arguing about the weight of whatever is made admissible.

The late Senator Kennedy of Massachusetts called these hearings a Supreme Court nominee's "job interview with the American people."

And by that standard, the nominee before us is coming into his job interview with more than 90% of his background hidden.

I would think that anyone who wanted to sit on the nation's highest court would be proud of their record and would want the American people to see it.

I would think that anyone privileged to be nominated to the Supreme Court of the Unites States would want to be confirmed in a process that is not under a cloud, that respects due process.

I would think that anyone nominated to the Supreme Court of the United States would want to have a hearing that is characterized by transparency and fairness and integrity and not shrouded by uncertainty and suspicion, and concealment and doubt.

We should not be moving forward with this hearing. The American people deserve better than this.

So Judge Kavanaugh, as most of us know, and I will mention to you and you have young children and I know they are very proud of you and I know you are a great parent and I applaud all that you have done in the community. And so as you know and we all know, this is a week when most students in our country go back to school.

And it occurs to me that many years ago, right around this time, I was starting kindergarten and I was in a bus, a school bus, on my way to Thousand Oaks Elementary School as part of the second class of students as busing desegregated Berkeley, California, public schools.

This was decades after the Supreme Court ruled Brown v. Board of Education that separate was inherently unequal.

And as I've said many times, had Chief Justice Earl Warren not been on the Supreme Court of the United States, he could not have led a unanimous decision and the outcome then of that case may have been very different.

Had that decision not come down the way it did, I may not have had the opportunities that allowed me to become a lawyer or a prosecutor.

I likely would not have been elected District Attorney of San Francisco or the Attorney General of California.

And I most certainly would not be sitting here as a member of the United States Senate.

So for me, a Supreme Court seat is not only about academic issues of legal precedent or judicial philosophy. It is personal.

When we talk about our nation's highest court, and the men and women who sit on it, we're talking about the impact that one individual on that Court can have. Impact on people you will never meet and whose names you will never know.

Whether a person can exercise their Constitutional right to cast a ballot may be decided if Judge Kavanaugh sits on that Court.

Whether a woman with breast cancer can afford healthcare or is forced off lifesaving treatment.

Whether a gay or transgender worker is treated with dignity or may be treated as a second-class citizen.

Whether a young woman who got pregnant at 15 is forced to give birth or in desperation go to a back alley for an abortion.

Whether a President of the United States can be held accountable or whether he'll be above the law.

All of this may come down to Judge Kavanaugh's vote.

And that's what's at stake in this nomination.

And the stakes are even higher because of the moment we're in, and many of us have discussed this. These are unprecedented times.

As others have already observed, less than 2 weeks ago, the President's personal lawyer and campaign chairman were each found guilty or pleaded guilty to 8 felonies.

The President's personal lawyer, under oath, declared that the President directed him to commit a federal crime.

Yet that same President is racing to appoint to a lifetime position on the highest court in our land, a court that very well may decide his legal fate.

And yes, that's essentially what confirming Judge Kavanaugh could mean.

So it is important, more important I'd say than ever, that the American people have transparency and accountability with this nomination.

And that's why it is extremely disturbing that Senate Republicans have prevented this body, and most important, the American people from fully reviewing Judge Kavanaugh's record, and have disregarded just about every tradition and practice that I heard so much about before I arrived in this place.

Judge Kavanaugh, when you and I met in my office, you said with respect to judicial decisions, that rushed decisions are often bad decisions.

I agree with you. I agree with you.

And when we are talking about who will sit on the Supreme Court of the United States, I believe your point couldn't be more important.

Mr. Chairman, when Judge Kavanaugh was nominated in July, he expressed his belief that "A judge must be independent and must interpret the law, not make the law."

But in reviewing this nominee's background, I am deeply concerned that what guides him is not independence or impartiality. It's not even ideology. I would suggest it is not even ideology.

What I believe guides him and what his record that we've been able to see shows, is what guides this nominee is partisanship.

This nominee has devoted his entire career to a conservative Republican agenda.

Helping to spearhead a partisan investigation into President Clinton.

Helping George W. Bush's legal team ensure that every vote was not counted in Bush v. Gore. Helping to confirm partisan judges and enact partisan laws as part of the Bush White House.

And in all of these efforts, he has shown that he seeks to win at all costs, even if that means pushing the envelope.

And if we look at his record on the D.C. Circuit, and in his recent writings and statements, it is clear that the nominee has brought his political bias to the bench.

He has carried out deeply conservative, partisan agenda as a judge, favoring big business over ordinary Americans, polluters over clean air and water, and the powerful over the vulnerable.

Just last year, Judge Kavanaugh praised the dissent in Roe v. Wade and ruled against a scared, 17-year-old girl seeking to end her pregnancy.

He has disregarded the Supreme Court precedent to argue that undocumented workers weren't really employees under our labor laws.

We have witnessed horrific mass shootings from Parkland to Las Vegas to Jacksonville, Florida.

Yet Judge Kavanaugh has gone further than the Supreme Court and has written that because assault weapons are in "common use," assault weapons and high-capacity magazines cannot be banned under the Second Amendment.

When he was part of an Independent Counsel investigation into the Democratic president, the nominee was dogged in demanding answers.

And yet, he has since changed his tune, arguing that presidents should not be investigated or held accountable, a position that I'm sure is not lost on this President.

These positions are not impartial, they are partisan.

Justice Neil Gorsuch, Judge Kavanaugh's classmate, insisted before this Committee that judges are not merely "politicians in robes." I fear that Judge Kavanagh's record indicates that is exactly what he may very well be.

Now, I know members of this Committee and the nominee's friends and colleagues have assured us that he is devoted to his family, and supportive of his law clerks, and volunteers in his community. And I don't doubt that at all.

But that's not why we are here. I'd rather that we think about this hearing, in the context of the Supreme Court of the United States, and the impact it will have on generations of Americans to come. And do we want that Court to continue a legacy of being above politics and unbiased? Or are we prepared to participate in a process that is tainted and that leaves the American public questioning the integrity of this process?

And I'll close by saying this. We have a system of justice that is symbolized by a statue of a woman holding scales. And she wears a blindfold.

Justice wears a blindfold because we have said in the United States of America, under our judicial system, justice should be blind to a person's status.

We have said that in our system of justice, justice should be blind to how much money someone has, to what you look like or who you love, to who your parents are and the language they speak.

And every Supreme Court Justice must understand and uphold that ideal.

And sir, should those cases come before you, Judge Kavanaugh, I am concerned whether you would treat every American equally or instead show allegiance to the political party and the conservative agenda that has shaped and built your career.

I am concerned your loyalty would be to the President who appointed you and not to the Constitution of the United States.

These concerns I hope you will answer during the course of this hearing. I believe the American people have a right to have these concerns. I also believe the American public has a right to full and candid answers to the questions that are presented to you during the course of this hearing. I will be paying of course very close attention to your testimony and I think you know, the American public will be paying very close attention to your testimony.

Thank you.

CNN September 6, 2018

Kavanaugh Questioned On Capitol Hill For Nearly 10 Hours Kavanaugh Takes Pointed Questions From Dems; Sen. Harris Questions Kavanaugh After Tense Exchange On Mueller

THIS IS A RUSH TRANSCRIPT. THIS COPY MAY NOT BE IN ITS FINAL FORM AND MAY BE UPDATED.

SEN. KAMALA HARRIS, (D) JUDICIARY COMMITEE: -- I have shared with you that other nominees sitting at that desk or some desk like that have committed to recusing. There have been circumstances where they have committed. So, is it your opinion then that they violated some ethical code or rule?

BRETT KAVANAUGH, SUPREME COURT NOMINEE: I don't know all the circumstances but I believe those were situations that were required recusals where they had previously had to recuse and were simply indicating their required recusals. But I don't know all the circumstances.

A discretionary recusal is a commitment to get a job or discretionary nonracial as a commitment to get a job, either direction, would be violating my independence as a judge, as a sitting judge and as a nominee to the court.

HARRIS: OK. It is clear you're unwilling at this point to commit to recusal so we can move on.

One of your mentors, Justice Kennedy, wrote landmark opinions in the area of LGBTQ rights that have had a major impact on the lives of many Americans. Let's discuss one of those cases and that's the Obergefell case. You know, Obergefell as you know the court held that same sex couples have a right to marry. My question is whether the Obergefell case was correctly decided in your opinion?

KAVANAUGH: Senator, Justice Kennedy wrote the majority opinion in a series of five cases, Romer v. Evans --

HARRIS: If we can just talk about Obergefell that would be great.

KAVANAUGH: I want to explain it.

HARRIS: I actually know the history leading up to Obergefell. So can you just please address your comments to Obergefell?

KAVANAUGH: So, I'd like to explain it if I can. He wrote the majority opinion in Romer v. Evans, Lawrence v. Texas, United States v. Windsor, Obergefell, and Masterpiece Cakeshop, concluding in Masterpiece Cakeshop, importantly, with a statement, if I could just read this --

HARRIS: No, please don't, because I actually have read it, and I'm sure most have. My question is very specific. Can you comment, on your personal opinion, on whether Obergefell was correctly decided? It's a yes or no. Please.

KAVANAUGH: In Masterpiece Cakeshop, and this is, I think, relevant to your question, Justice Kennedy wrote, in the majority opinion joined by Chief Justice Roberts, and Justice Alito, and Justice Gorsuch, and Justice Breyer, and Justice Kagan, the days of discriminating against gay and lesbian Americans, or treating gay and lesbian Americans as inferior in dignity and worth, are over, to paraphrase him.

HARRIS: Do you agree with that statement?

KAVANAUGH: That is the precedent of the Supreme Court agreed with by --

HARRIS: You, sir. I'm asking your opinion. You're the nominee right now, and so it is probative of your ability to serve on the highest court in our land. So I'm asking you a very specific question. Either you're willing to answer it or not, and if you're not willing to answer it, we can move on. But do you believe Obergefell was correctly decided?

KAVANAUGH: So, each of the justices have declined, as a matter of judicial independence, each of them, to answer questions in that line of cases.

HARRIS: So you will not answer that question?

KAVANAUGH: Following the precedent set by those eight justices, they've all declined when asked to answer that question.

HARRIS: Thank you. I have limited time.

KAVANAUGH: But it's important be --

HARRIS: I'd really like to move on. You've said that Brown v. Board of Education was one of the greatest moments in the court's history. Do you believe that Obergefell was also one of those moments?

KAVANAUGH: I've said, Senator, consistent with what the nominees have done, that the vast swath of modern case law, as Justice

Kagan put it, you can't as a nominee in this seat give a thumbs up or thumbs down. That was -- that's her word.

HARRIS: Do you think that Obergefell was one of the great moments in the history of the Supreme Court of the United States?

KAVANAUGH: And for that reason those nominees have declined to comment on reasons cases, all of them.

HARRIS: Is it a great moment is what I'm asking you. Not to comment on the legal analysis. Do you believe that was a great moment in the history of the court?

KAVANAUGH: Justice Kennedy wrote the majority opinion saying the days of treating gay and lesbian Americans, or gay and lesbian couples, as second-class citizens or inferior in dignity or worth are over in the Supreme Court. That's a very important statement, Senator.

HARRIS: I agree. That's why I think you repeated it. Thank you.

Let's move on. Over the last several months we have all witnessed the inhumane and heartbreaking separation of immigrant children from their families by this administration. Despite a court order requiring the administration to reunite them over a month ago, nearly 500 immigrant children are still separated from their parents. Do you believe that constitutional rights of parents, specifically fundamental due process rights are implicated in such family separations?

[19:04:59] KAVANAUGH: Senator, that is a matter of pending litigation I believe and as a sitting judge on the D.C. circuit or as a nominee, I of course can't comment.

HARRIS: Have you watched the coverage of any of these cases on television or have you read about the experience those parents and those children have had?

KAVANAUGH: I have seen some television.

HARRIS: In the 1889 Chinese exclusion case, the Supreme Court permitted a ban on Chinese people entering the United States. The court said the Chinese people are "impossible to assimilate with our people," and said they were immigrating in numbers, "approaching an invasion." This case has never been explicitly overruled. You've said you'd be willing to talk about older cases, so can you tell me, was the United States Supreme Court correct in holding that Chinese people could be banned from entering our country?

KAVANAUGH: Senator, the cases in the 1890s as you know --

HARRIS: 1889 to be specific.

KAVANAUGH: OK. In that era reflect discriminatory attitudes by the Supreme Court. Of course, that's the era also of Plessy v. Ferguson.

HARRIS: So would you be willing to say that was incorrectly decided?

KAVANAUGH: Senator, I don't want to opine on a case -- particular case without looking at it and studying the discrimination.

HARRIS: Are you aware that that case has not been overturned?

KAVANAUGH: Senator, I know that with a number of the cases like Korematsu -- let me use that as an example.

HARRIS: Which we've discussed earlier. But in this particular case in particular, were you aware that it had not been overturned

KAVANAUGH: Senator, I realized that there's still cases in the immigration context --

HARRIS: Have you ever written about any of those cases and your thoughts about whether they should be re-examined or potentially overturned and sometimes obviously they should be overturned?
KAVANAUGH: Well, there is a swath of cases.

HARRIS: Have you talked about this case ever?

KAVANAUGH: I do not -- I do not believe. I'm happy to be refreshed if you have something that suggests I have.

HARRIS: No, it's actually a question.

KAVANAUGH: OK.

HARRIS: And under the constitution, Judge, do you believe that Congress or the president can ban entry into the United tates on the basis of race?

KAVANAUGH: Senator, that was of course one of the issues that was just in litigation and there's still litigation about the immigration laws and how exclusions --

HARRIS: You're not going to answer that?

KAVANAUGH: That's pending litigation so I think I as a matter of independence and precedent --

HARRIS: Will not answer that. That's fine. Let's move on. In 2013 Texas passed a law that imposed new restrictions on health care facilities that provide abortions. The effect was that after the law was passed, half of those facilities closed which severely limited access to health care for the women of Texas.

In 2016, Whole Woman's Health was decided where in the Supreme Court invalidated the Texas restrictions. Was Whole Woman's Health correctly decided? Yes or no. And we can keep it short and move on.

KAVANAUGH: Senator, consistent with the approach of nominees --

HARRIS: You will not be answering that?

KAVANAUGH: -- following that nominee precedent.

HARRIS: OK. I'd like to ask you another question which I believe you can answer. You've said repeatedly that Roe v. Wade is an important precedent. I'd like to understand what that really means for the lives of women. We've had a lot of conversations about how the discussion we're having in this room will impact real people out there.

And so my question is what in your opinion is still unresolved? For example, can a state prevent a woman from using the most common or widely accept medical procedure to terminate her pregnancy? Do you believe that that is still an unresolved issue? I'm not asking how you would decide it.

KAVANAUGH: So I don't want to comment on hypothetical cases. Roe v. Wade is an important precedent. It's been reaffirmed many times.

HARRIS: So are you willing to say that it would be unconstitutional for a state to place such a restriction on women for Roe v. Wade?

KAVANAUGH: Senator, you can -- the precedent of the Supreme Court was -- in Roe was reaffirmed in Planned Parenthood v. Casey of course and that's precedent on precedent and then there a lot of cases applying the undue burden standard and those themselves are important precedence and I have to apply them --

HARRIS: And we've discussed that many times. So I've actually had the benefit of sitting through most of the hours of your testimony the last two days.

KAVANAUGH: Thank you.

HARRIS: I know you've talked a lot about that. Can Congress ban abortions nationwide after 20 weeks of pregnancy?

KAVANAUGH: Senator, that would require me to comment on potential legislation that I understand and, therefore, I shouldn't as a matter of judicial independence following the precedent of nominees --

HARRIS: OK. And we can move on. I'm going to ask you about unenumerated rights.

[19:10:00] So you gave a speech praising former Justice Rehnquist's dissent in Roe. There's been much discussion about that and you wrote "celebrating his successes stemming the general tide of free willing judicial creation of unenumerated rights." That is what you said in celebration of Justice Rehnquist.

So unenumerated rights is a phrase that lawyers used, but I want to make clear what we're talking about. It means rights that are protected by the constitution even if they're not specifically mentioned in the constitution. So they're net book that you carry.

So what we're talking about is the right to vote. That's an unenumerated right, the right to have children, the right to control children, the right to control the upbringing of your children, the right to refuse medical care, the right to love the partner of your choice, the right to marry, and the right to have an abortion.

Now putting those unenumerated rights in the context of the statement you made, which was to praise the stemming of the general tide of freewheeling creation of unenumerated rights, which means you were -- the interpretation there is you were praising this quest to end those unenumerated rights. My question to you is which of the rights that I just mentioned do you want to put an end to or roll back?

KAVANAUGH: Three points, I believe, Senator. First, the constitution, it is in the book that I carry. The constitution protects unenumerated rights, that's what the Supreme Court has said.

HARRIS: But that does not explicitly protect the rights that I just listed in. And we both know that that's the case.

KAVANAUGH: Right. So that's point one. Point two is Glucksberg, the case you're referring to, specifically cited Planned Parenthood v. Casey as authority in that case. So Casey reaffirmed Roe. Casey is cited as authority in Glucksberg, that's point two. And point three, Justice Kagan when she sat in this chair pointed repeatedly to Glucksberg as the test for recognizing unenumerated rights going forward. I, in describing the president, I agree with her description of that in her hearing.

HARRIS: So -- thank you for that. So then let's put the rights that I mentioned which are unenumerated in the context of your praise of Justice Rehnquist as having stemmed the general tide of freewheeling judicial creation of unenumerated rights. Arguably, every rights that I mentioned on that list was a judicially created unenumerated right. And my question then is when you praise a jurist who attempted to end those rights, which rights in particular do you believe are praiseworthy of ending?

KAVANAUGH: Right. So that was the test that was set forth by the Supreme Court going forward for recognition of additional unenumerated rights. That was cited as authority in that case, Planned Parenthood v. Casey, which reaffirmed Roe.

HARRIS: So let's talk about the right to vote. Do you believe that that falls in the category of having been caught up in the general tide of freewheeling judicial creation of unenumerated rights?

KAVANAUGH: What I was describing with Chief Justice Rehnquist and it was that description of his career was in a variety of areas. And his role --

HARRIS: Specifically, the reference was to unenumerated rights.

KAVANAUGH: Right. And in a number of areas I've described five different areas of jurisprudence where he had helped the Supreme Court achieved what I think has been a common sense middle ground that stood the test of time in terms of precedent in a variety of areas that resets how others have described it.

The Glucksberg case, as Justice Kagan explained when she was in this chair, is the case that the Supreme Court has relied on for forward looking future of recognition of unenumerated rights.

HARRIS: Thank you, sir. I'm familiar with that. I think you're not going to address the specific unenumerated rights or are you? Because if not, we can move on.

KAVANAUGH: I think I've addressed it. Thank you, Senator.

HARRIS: OK. In 2011 you were a judge on of the challenges to the Affordable Care Act. The court you sat upon held -- you dissented on procedural grounds on the court which upheld the act. One of your former law clerks described your opinion in that case, and that's the seventh sky case as, "a thorough takedown of the individual mandate." He would go on to clerk for Supreme Court

Justice Kennedy that year or the next year and the Supreme Court then held -- or heard the challenge of the Affordable care act.

And according to him, your opinion was "roadmap" for the dissenting justices, the ones who would have struck down the Affordable Care Act. Given you wrote the "roadmap," according to your law clerk, could one reasonably conclude that you would have voted to strike down the Affordable Care Act had you been on be the Supreme Court?

[19:15:06] KAVANAUGH: Couple of points, Senator. First, I concluded -- in one case, I upheld the Affordable Care Act against an Origination Clause challenge. In the case you're referring to, I did not reach the merits but I discussed the merits pro that were being argued in both directions. My opinion has been described as the roadmap for both sides because I described both positions. And actually it wasn't a roadmap at all because I didn't reach --

HARRIS: You also described it as a takedown.

KAVANAUGH: Well, I speak for myself and my own opinions speak for themselves.

HARRIS: It was out of bounds. Chairman wants to close this questioning so we can leave it with that. Thank you, Judge.

KAVANAUGH: Thank you for your time, Senator.

~~~~~~~~~~~~~~~~~~~~~~~~~~~~~~~~~~~~~

https://transcripts.cnn.com/show/ebo/date/2018-09-06/segment/01

OPEN HEARING ON FOREIGN INFLUENCE OPERATIONS'
USE OF SOCIAL MEDIA PLATFORMS
(COMPANY WITNESSES)

HEARING BEFORE THE SELECT COMMITTEE ON
INTELLIGENCE OF THE UNITED STATES SENATE
ONE HUNDRED FIFTEENTH CONGRESS
SECOND SESSION

WEDNESDAY, SEPTEMBER 5, 2018

Pg 46 – 49

Chairman BURR. Senator Harris.

Senator HARRIS. Thank you, Mr. Chairman, for accommodating me. I'm in another hearing as you know. Good morning, and to the invisible witness, good morning to you. So I have a few questions for Ms. Sandberg. On November 2, 2017, your company's general counsel testified in front of this Intelligence Committee on Russian interference, and I asked a few questions.

I asked how much money did you make, and this is of the representative from both Facebook and Twitter—both of your general counsels were here. And I asked how much money did you make from legitimate advertising that ran alongside the Russian propaganda. The Twitter general counsel said, quote, "We haven't done the analysis but we'll follow-up with you and work on that." And the Facebook general counsel said the same is true for Facebook.

Again, I asked Facebook CEO Mark Zuckerberg on April 10, 2018, and he said that, quote, "Internet Research Agency, the Russian firm, ran about $100,000 worth of ads." Following the hearing, I asked Facebook the same question in writing, and on June 8, 2018, we received a response that said, quote, "We believe the annual revenue that is attributable to inauthentic or false accounts is immaterial."

So my question is: What did you mean by immaterial? Because I'm a bit confused about the use of that term in this context.

Ms. SANDBERG. Thank you for the question.

Again we believe the total of the ad spending that we have found is about $100,000. And so the question you're asking is with the inorganic content, I believe, what is the possible revenue we could have made? So here's the best way I can think of to estimate that, which is that we believe between 2015 and 2017, up to 150 million people may have seen the IRA ads or organic content in our serv-ice. And the way our service works is, ads don't run attached to any specific piece of content, but they're scattered throughout the content. This is equivalent to .004 percent of content in news feed and that was why they would say it was immaterial to our earnings.

But I really want to say that from our point of view, Senator Harris, any amount is too much.

Senator HARRIS. If I may, just so I'm clear about your response— so are you saying that then the revenue generated was .004 per-cent of your annual revenue? Of course that would not be immaterial.

Ms. SANDBERG. Again, the ads are not attached to any piece of content so

Senator HARRIS. So what metric then? Just help me with that. What metric are you using to calculate the revenue that was generated, associated with those ads? And what is the dollar amount that is associated then with that metric?

Ms. SANDBERG. The reason we can't answer the question to your satisfaction is that ads are not—organic content—ads don't run with inorganic content on our service, so there is actually no way to firmly ascertain how much ads are attached to how much organic content. It's not how it works.

In trying to answer what percentage of the organic——

Senator HARRIS. But what percentage of the content on Facebook is inorganic?

Ms. SANDBERG. I don't have that specific answer, but we can come back to you with that.

Senator HARRIS. Would you say it's the majority?

Ms. SANDBERG. No. No.

Senator HARRIS. An insignificant amount? What percentage? You must know.

Ms. SANDBERG. If you ask about our inauthentic accounts on Facebook, we believe at any point in time it's 3 percent to 4 percent of accounts, but that's not the same answer as inorganic content because some accounts generate more content than others.

Senator HARRIS. I agree. So what percentage of your content is inorganic?

Ms. SANDBERG. Again, we don't know. I can follow up with the answer to that.

Senator HARRIS. Okay, please. That would be great. And then your company's business model is obviously—it's complex but benefits from increased user engagement and that results of course in increased revenue. So, simply put, the more people that use your platform, the more they are exposed to third-party ads, the more revenue you generate. Would you agree with that?

Ms. SANDBERG. Can you repeat? I just want to make sure I got it exactly right.

Senator HARRIS. So the more user engagement will result—and the more then that they are exposed to third-party ads—the more that will increase your revenue. So the more users that are on your platform—

Ms. SANDBERG. Yes. Yes. But only I think when they see really authentic content. Because I think in the short run and over the long run it doesn't benefit us to have anything inauthentic on our platform.

Senator HARRIS. That makes sense. In fact, the first quarter of 2018, the number of daily active users on Facebook rose 13 percent, I'm told. And corresponding ad revenue grew by half to $11.79 billion. Does that sound correct to you?

Ms. SANDBERG. Sounds correct.

Senator HARRIS. And then would you agree that—I think it's an obvious point—that the more people that engage on the platform, the more potential there is for revenue generation for Facebook?

Ms. SANDBERG. Yes, Senator. But again, only when the content is authentic.

Senator HARRIS. I appreciate that point. And so a concern that many have is how you can reconcile an incentive to create and increase your user engagement when the content that generates a lot of engagement is often inflammatory and hateful.

So, for example, Lisa-Maria Neudert, a researcher at Oxford and Internet Institute, says, quote, ''The content that is the most mis-leading or conspiratorial, that's what's generating the most discussion and the most engagement, and that's what the algorithm is designed to respond to.''

My concern is that according to Facebook's community standards, you do not allow hate speech on Facebook. However, contrary to what we've seen, on June 28, 2017, a ProPublica report found that Facebook's training materials instructed reviewers to delete hate speech targeting white men but not against black children because black children are not a protected class. Do you know anything about that, and can you talk to me about that?

Ms. SANDBERG. I do. And what that was, I think, a bad policy that's been changed, but it wasn't saying that black children—it was saying that children—it was saying that different groups weren't looked at the same way, and we've fixed it.

Senator HARRIS. But isn't that the concern with hate, period? That not everyone is looked at the same way?

Ms. SANDBERG. Well, hate speech is against our policies and we take strong measures to take it down. We also publish publicly what our hate speech standards are. We care tremendously about civil rights. We have worked very closely with civil rights groups to find hate speech on our platform and take it down.

Senator HARRIS. So when did you address that policy? I'm glad to hear you have. When was that addressed?

Ms. SANDBERG. When it came out—and again, that policy was a badly written, bad example, and not a real policy.

Senator HARRIS. The report that I'm aware of was from June of 2017. Was the policy changed after that report or before that report from ProPublica?

Ms. SANDBERG. I can get back to you on the specifics of when that would have happened.

Senator HARRIS. You're not aware of when it happened?

Ms. SANDBERG. I don't remember the exact date.

Senator HARRIS. Do you remember the year?

Ms. SANDBERG. Well, you just said it was 2017.

Senator HARRIS. So do you believe it was 2017 that the policy changed?

Ms. SANDBERG. It sounds like it was.

Senator HARRIS. Okay. And what is Facebook's official stance on then hate speech regarding so-called, and legally defined, unprotected classes, such as children?

Ms. SANDBERG. Hate speech is not allowed on our platform and hate speech is, you know, important in every way. And we care a lot that our platform is a safe community. When people come to Facebook to share, they're coming because they want to connect on the issues that matter to them.

Senator HARRIS. So, have you removed the requirement that you will only protect with your hate speech policy those classes of people that have been designated as protected classes in a legal context? Is that no longer the policy of Facebook?

Ms. SANDBERG. I know that our hate speech policies go beyond the legal classifications and they are all public and we can get back to you on any of that. It's all publicly available.

Senator HARRIS. Thank you so much. Thank you, Mr. Chairman.